The Monkey & the Wrench

The Monkey & the Wrench

Essays into Contemporary Poetics

Mary Biddinger and John Gallaher, Editors
Nick Sturm, Associate Editor

The University of Akron Press
Akron, Ohio

All rights reserved · First Edition 2011 · Manufactured in the United States of America. · All inquiries and permission requests should be addressed to the Publisher, the University of Akron Press, Akron, Ohio 44325-1703.

15   14   13   12   11   5   4   3   2   1

LIBRARY OF CONGRESS CATALOGING-IN-PUBLICATION DATA
The monkey and the wrench : essays into contemporary poetics / Mary Biddinger and John Gallaher, editors. — 1st ed.
p. cm. — (Akron series in contemporary poetics)
Includes bibliographical references and index.
ISBN 978-1-931968-91-1 (pbk. : alk. paper)
1. Poetics—History—20th century. 2. Poetics—History—21st century. 3. American poetry—20th century—History and criticism. 4. American poetry—21st century—History and criticism. I. Biddinger, Mary. II. Gallaher, John, 1965–
PN1042.M57 2011
808.1—DC22

                          2010047973

The paper used in this publication meets the minimum requirements of American National Standard for Information Sciences—Permanence of Paper for Printed Library Materials, ANSI Z39.48-1984. ∞

The views contained herein are those of the individual authors, and do not necessarily reflect the views of the editors, the Akron Series in Contemporary Poetics, or The University of Akron Press.

Cover design by Amy Freels. Cover: *Untitled*. Copyright © 2008 by Amy Freels, used with permission.
The Monkey and the Wrench was designed and typeset by Amy Freels. The typeface, Mrs. Eaves, was designed by Zuzana Licko in 1996. The display type, Brandon Grotesque, was designed by Hannes von Döhren in 2009/10. *The Monkey and the Wrench* was printed on sixty-pound natural and bound by BookMasters of Ashland, Ohio.

Contents

Introduction
Of Monkeys and Wrenches

Mary Biddinger and John Gallaher

C oming up with a title for this collection caused us great consternation. Monkey see, monkey do. Throw a monkey wrench in the works. Monkey mind. Don't monkey with it. Hundredth monkey effect. Infinite monkey theorem. No more monkeys jumping on the bed. A barrel full of monkeys, etc. And then what happens?

There's a long history of monkey metaphors, as well as wrench metaphors, so as soon as our Associate Editor, Nick Sturm, suggested "The Monkey and the Wrench," we leapt at it. It is a fine way to encapsulate our thinking behind putting this collection together, that there are many ways into contemporary poetry and poetics, and that we wanted to provide a forum for some writers to tinker with it.

We wanted a book that might prove as useful to readers of poetry as it would be to poets, and, as well, as interesting for students as it would be to general readers. We share the feeling about poetry that we're all in this together as readers, writers, critics, students, and teachers. We're all of the above in the face of art. And to deny any of these roles is to deny a fundamental way that art works upon and with us. The essays in this volume, then, are not meant to stake out a territory or to advance a singular aesthetic position. Nor do we see this volume as definitive. These are open questions, beginnings or continuances of conversations around and in contemporary poetry, not manifestos or final words. We saw this as our goal.

We chose these authors (with a few exceptions, which we'll get to in a bit) without knowing what they were going to take as the specific subjects of their essays. We wanted to know what they were interested in, to let the contents lead the collection. Eclecticism was our hope, and we've been rewarded. Give enough monkeys a wrench, as the saying goes that we just made up. The wrench—both the way to fix something and the way one might throw it into the works. The monkey—both James Tate's "Teaching the Ape to Write Poems" and Thomas Lux's "Helping the Monkey Cross the River." We're all in this together, helping the monkey along.

If we're doing it right, we inhabit art as a part of the encounter, to paraphrase one of our teachers, Wayne Dodd, who illustrated, through his presence with a text, how it's not reading we're doing, but living into. Texts are experiences, and this is serious stuff, worth taking seriously, which also includes an open field for the antic. *Attend,* is what art calls out to us. What, if anything, art owes us, is another thing. Sometimes in this encounter it's enough to point, and sometimes it's imperative to point out.

Beware monkeys with wrenches. You never know what they'll do. And so what has been done here?

The collection opens with a bit of context. By historically unraveling poetry's relationship with the reading public, Robert Archambeau, in "The Discursive Situation of Poetry," deconstructs the contemporary argument that American poetry is out of touch with its audience, and reconceptualizes the issue in the face of larger and farther-reaching trends. From that moment of history, we move to "The Moves: Common Maneuvers in Contemporary Poetry," where Elisa Gabbert revisits a topic that was popular on the internet last year. Gabbert, along with Mike Young, investigated some of the common compositional practices and ticks of twenty-first century American poetry on the website HTML GIANT. We asked her to work part of it up for this volume, and we were pleased that she sent it to us.

Just as important as the common moves in poetry are the less common ones. Michael Dumanis's essay, "An Aesthetics of Accumulation: On the Contemporary Litany" discusses the popularity of litany in contemporary poetry, highlighting litany's sonic qualities as well as how it establishes a unified framework on which even a poem consisting of fragmentary elements can be built. The investigation of less common moves in contemporary poetry continues as Stephen Burt's "Cornucopia, or, Contemporary American Rhyme" takes up the topic of rhyme. Burt examines the technical and aesthetic principles of rhyme in English over the centuries, and then focuses on its use by contemporary American poets.

Suspicious of the sacredness of what is "original," Benjamin Paloff, in "I Am One of an Infinite Number of Monkeys Named Shakespeare, or; Why I Don't Own this Language," advocates for a continual rethinking and subversive reimagining of meaning and completeness in poetry, arguing that all poetry is a kind of translation, a transformation of thought, a blasphemous and necessary risk. Staying in this realm a moment longer, in "Persona and the Mystical Poem," Elizabeth Robinson explores the mystical poem, defining "mystical" information not necessarily as religious or divine experience, but as that which defies conventional logic. Robinson engages the notion of speaker and persona in this paper, and cites the work of numerous poets, including Jean Grosjean (Keith Waldrop, tran.) and Jack Spicer.

In the next essay, "A Wilderness of Monkeys," the second piece to mention monkeys in the title, and thereby making us feel some sort of monkey title was in order, David Kirby addresses the power of indistinctness, and invokes a variety of art forms and artists, from Shakespeare to Johnny Cash. Kirby argues that a lack of concrete imagery in art is just as, if not more, gripping than continual direct reference to meaning and intention.

At the AWP convention in Denver, we attended a panel titled "Hybrid Aesthetics and its Discontents," which brought several criticisms of the anthology *American Hybrid* together. As *American Hybrid* was both highly praised and highly criticized, and as Cole Swensen, one of the editors, talked about it as a way to start a conversation, we contacted the panel organizer, Michael Theune, about including it in this volume. After talking with the other panelists, Arielle Greenberg, Craig Santos Perez, Megan Volpert, and Mark Wallace, Theune sent it to us. Since this was now a fully involved conversation, we thought it would be a good idea to contact Cole Swensen for a response, and she generously replied with her "Response to Hybrid Aesthetics and its Discontents."

We felt it was fitting for us to have this symposium and response from Cole Swensen in this, our first volume, because it illustrates our vision in putting this collection together, which is that we're not looking for essays that agree with each other (or with us), but essays that are investigating poetry and the situation of poetry as something important, and with something at stake. We tried to get some of that feeling in the title, by having "Essays into Contemporary Poetics" as our subtitle. That "into" was important to us. It's not *in*, it's *into*. Anyway, those were the sorts of things we were thinking about.

In a fitting move, we saved "Goodbye, Goodbye, Goodbye: Notes on the Ends of Poems" by Joy Katz for the end. In it, Katz examines the musical and traditional roots of repetition, while suggesting various alternative poetic closure techniques available to contemporary poets.

Concluding with really concluding, we look forward to the future conversations that these essays will certainly be a part of, as well as what might happen next in this series. The doctor said, as we all know, "No more monkeys jumping on the bed." But doctors don't know *everything*.

We'd like to thank Thomas Bacher, Amy Freels, and Carol Slatter at the University of Akron Press for their tremendous support for this project. We also wish to thank our Akron Series in Contemporary Poetics editorial board for helping us to conceptualize this project: Maxine Chernoff, Martha Collins, Kevin Prufer, Alissa Valles, and G. C. Waldrep.

Special thanks to Associate Editor of the Akron Series in Contemporary Poetics Nick Sturm, and to the band of talented Assistant Editors for this project: Michelle Skupski Bissell, Susan Grimm, Michael Krutel, Eric Morris, and Samuel Snodgrass. We'd also like to thank Curt Brown, Alexis Pope, and Jay Robinson for their editorial contributions to this project.

This monkey, as they say, has gone to heaven.

The Discursive Situation of Poetry

Robert Archambeau

"Why *do* poets continue to write? Why keep playing if it's such a mug's game? Some, no doubt, simply fail to understand the situation."
—SVEN BIRKERTS

The important point to notice, though, is this:
  Each poet knew for whom he had to write,
Because their life was still the same as his.
  As long as art remains a parasite
  On any class of persons it's alright;
The only thing it must be is attendant,
The only thing it mustn't, independent.
—W. H. AUDEN

Statistics confirm what many have long suspected: poetry is being read by an ever-smaller slice of the American reading public. Poets and critics who have intuited this have blamed many things, but for the most part they have blamed the rise of MFA programs in creative writing. While they have made various recommendations on how to remedy the situation, these remedies are destined for failure or, at best, for very limited success, because the rise of MFA programs is merely a symptom of much larger and farther-reaching trends. These trends are unlikely to be reversed by the intervention of a few poets, critics, and arts-administrators. I'm not sure this is a bad thing. Or, in any event, I'm not sure it is worse than what a reversal of the decline in readership would entail. Let me explain.

Decades of Complaint

While we don't have many instruments for measuring the place of poetry in American life, all our instruments agree: poetry has been dropping precipitously in popularity for some time. In 1992, the National Endowment for the Arts conducted a survey that concluded only 17.1% of those who read books had read any poetry in the previous year. A similar N.E.A. survey published in 2002 found that the figure had declined to 12.1%. The N.E.A. numbers for 2008 were grimmer still: only 8.3% of book readers had read any poetry in the survey period (Bain). The portion of readers who read any poetry at all has, it seems, been cut in half over sixteen years. Poetry boosters can't help but be distressed by the trend.

Poets and poetry lovers have somewhat less faith in statistics and rather more faith in intuition and personal observation than the population at large. They've intuited this state of affairs for more than two decades, beginning long before the statistical trend became clear in all its stark, numerical reality. As far back as 1983, Donald Hall sounded a warning note in his essay "Poetry and Ambition." Although he did not blame the rise of the graduate creative writing programs for the loss of connection with an audience, he did feel that MFA programs created certain formal similarity among poems. The programs produced "McPoets," writing "McPoems" that were brief, interchangeable, and unambitious. His solution, delivered with tongue firmly in cheek, was to abolish MFA programs entirely. "What a ringing slogan for a new Cato," wrote Hall, "*Iowa delenda est!*" (Hall). Five years later Joseph Epstein picked up Hall's standard, and carried it further. In the incendiary essay "Who Killed Poetry?" Epstein argued that the rise of writing poems led not only to diminishments of ambition and quality—it furthered the decline of poetry's audience. The popular audience for poetry may have shrunk by the 1950s, argued Epstein, but at least the poets of midcentury were revered, and engaged with the larger intellectual world. By the late 1980s, though, poetry existed in "a vacuum." And what was the nature of this vacuum? "I should say that it consists of this," wrote Epstein, "it is scarcely read." Indeed, he continues,

> Contemporary poetry is no longer a part of the regular intellectual diet. People of general intellectual interests who feel that they ought to read or at least know about works on modern society or recent history or novels that attempt to convey something about the way we live now, no longer feel the same compunction about contemporary poetry. . . . It begins to seem, in fact, a sideline activity, a little as chiropractic or acupuncture is to mainstream medicine—odd, strange, but with a small cult of followers who swear by it. (Epstein)

The principle culprit in the sidelining of poetry was, for Epstein, the credentialing and employment of poets in graduate writing programs. "Whereas one tended to think of the modern poet as an artist," argued Epstein, "one tends to think of the contemporary poet as a professional," and, "like a true professional, he is insulated within the world of his fellow-professionals" (Epstein). The poet, instead of responding to the audience-driven world of the book market, responds only to his peers, *with the effect that the audience simply melts away.*

Après Epstein, *le déluge.* The 1990s saw a phalanx of poets and critics complaining about the decline of poetry's audience, and linking this decline to the rise of MFA programs. Dana Gioia fired the loudest shot in *Can Poetry Matter?* (published as an article in *The Atlantic* in 1991, republished in book form a year later). "American poetry now belongs to a subculture," said Gioia, "no longer part of the mainstream of intellectual life, it has become the specialized occupation of a relatively small and isolated group" (1). While he allows that they have done so "unwittingly," it is "the explosion of academic writing programs" that is to blame for this sad state of affairs, as far as Gioia is concerned (2). Gioia was by no means alone in this opinion. Vernon Shetley's 1993 study *After the Death of Poetry: Poet and Audience in Contemporary America* tells us that poetry has "lost the attention not merely of common readers but of intellectuals" (3)—and that creative writing programs have contributed to this loss by cultivating "a disturbing complacency" and by a "narrowing of the scope" of poetry (19). Bruce Bawer introduces his 1995 book of criticism, *Prophets and Professors,* by lamenting the professionalizing of poetry. He tells us that "those who read poetry— which, in our society, basically means poets" shy away from being too critical of the art, since "they conside[r] poetry so ailing and marginal a genre that criticism was . . . like kicking an invalid" (8). In the same year, Thomas Disch claimed in *The Castle of Indolence* that "for most readers . . . contemporary poetry might as well not exist." The reason, he says, is

> . . . that the workshops, which have a monopoly on the training of poets, encourage indolence, incompetence, smugness, and—most perniciously—that sense of victimization and special entitlement that poets now come to share with other artists who depend on government or institutional patronage to sustain their art, pay their salaries, and provide for their vacations. (5)

Blaming writing programs for the isolation of poetry extended beyond the fairly conservative literary preserves inhabited by the likes of Bawer, Disch, and Epstein. Charles Bernstein's 1995 essay "Warning—Poetry Area: Publics Under Construction," argues "it is bad for poetry, and for poets, to be nourished so disproportionately" by universities, adding that "the sort of poetry I care for has its natural habitat in the streets and offices and malls" (Bernstein).

By 1999, the chorus had grown so loud that Christopher Beach claimed we were "discussing the death of poetry to death" (19). Not that this stopped anyone. In 2006, Poetry Foundation President John Barr caused a stir with "American Poetry in the New Century," an article in *Poetry* magazine in which he noted poetry's "striking absence from the public dialogues of our day," as a sign that we have a reading public "in whose mind poetry is missing and unmissed." The problem, he asserts, stems from the writing programs. These produce poets who "write for one another," producing "a poetry that is neither robust, resonant, nor . . . entertaining." It cannot exist without "academic subsidies" and fails in the market, unable to sell in "commercial quantities" (Barr). While Barr surveys the terrain from the heights of the Poetry Foundation offices above Chicago, more recently the poet Daniel Nester has come to similar conclusions (albeit without the invocation of the values of the marketplace) from the depths of New York's poetry scene. Nester has characterized that scene as the product of the writing programs. Looking around at poetry events, he says he'd see university cliques such as the "Group of People Who Went to Iowa" and those starting "Teaching Jobs Out West." The scene was isolated from a larger engagement with society, with "a lack of connection to the reader" and readings attended only by "other aspiring poets" (Nester 2009). "It's an unsustainable system," he said when asked by an interviewer about his article. "Even the most niche of niche art forms has an audience. Not so with contemporary poetry" (Nester 2010).

As even this brief and incomplete survey of writers makes clear, American poets have noted the decline of the audience for poetry, and found it troubling. But when decriers of the decline make MFA programs their whipping boy they misunderstand the role such programs play in the distancing of poet from audience. In fact, poetry's decline of popularity predates the rise of writing programs, and such programs are properly seen as the latest episode in a larger and long-enduring drama, a drama that began in the nineteenth century.

Bohemia Misunderstood

Both Dana Gioia and Joseph Epstein contrast the contemporary situation with what they imagine to be better times for poets: for Gioia, the golden age took place in the 1940s, while for Epstein it took place a decade later.

What is most immediately striking about Gioia's imagined halcyon days for poetry is the strange combination of market-driven values and the idea of bohemia. The whole apparatus of poetry in the 1940s was, in Gioia's view, based on meeting consumer demand. In the 1940s, says Gioia, poets wrote with the idea of reaching a general readership, and "a poem that didn't command the reader's attention wasn't considered much of a poem." Editors of poetry journals looked to the market when determining their choices, not picking poems that met their own particular aesthetic standards, but choosing "verse that they felt would appeal to their particular audiences" (7). The problem since the professionalization of poetry has, for Gioia, been that "a poetry industry has been created to serve the interests of the producers and not the consumers" (10). Even critical judgment was bent to this end, as "the reviewers of fifty years ago knew that their primary loyalty must lie not with their fellow poets ... but with the reader" (16). Such conditions continued only so long as poets remained outside of an organized profession, and a preponderance of them "centered their lives in urban bohemias" (12).

Gioia's idea of a market-driven bohemia is, to put it mildly, singular. One can find nothing like it in the annals of the sociology of bohemian life and art. The standard view is that bohemia emerges in response to the marginalization of artists, poets, and other creative producers. Cesar Graña's classic study *Bohemian vs. Bourgeois*, for example, finds the origin of bohemia in the economic dislocations following the destruction of the aristocracy in the French Revolution. These dislocations led to a migration into urban centers of a "large marginal population" of educated people formerly connected to, or dependent on the aristocracy. Here they worked in opposition to, or at best on the fringes of, the market-driven world of the bourgeoisie (39). Albert Parry argues in *Garrets and Pretenders* that bohemia can only exist when there is an overproduction of certain kinds of skills and talents in relation to market demand for those skills. Pierre Bourdieu has famously defined the world of artistic production, especially as it involves poetry or occurs under bohemian conditions, as "the economic world reversed" (29). "The literary or artistic field," says Bourdieu, "is at all times the site of a struggle between the two principles of hierarchization: the heteronomous principle, favorable to those who dominate the field economically (e.g. 'bourgeois art') and the autonomous principle (e.g. 'art for art's sake')" (41). The heteronomous principle—that art should serve a force outside itself, such as the market—is certainly the force Gioia saw at work prior to the rise of writing programs. But the heteronomous principle is not the dominant force at work in the poetic and bohemian worlds. In such conditions, says Bourdieu, "the economy of practices is based, as in a generalized game of 'loser wins,' on a systematic inversion of all ordinary economies" including that of the market, because "it excludes the pursuit of profit and does not guarantee any sort of correspondence between investments and monetary gains" (39).

Validation for the poet, under bohemian conditions, cannot come in any great measure from the support of the market. Indeed, as Parry and Graña point out, bohemia comes into existence because there is too much literary and artistic talent for the market to absorb. In the absence of market support, poets do not seek to command the attention of a large readership for a sense of their worth. Rather, they start to seek validation from one another, and from a literary community separate from the broad, commercially profitable marketplace of readers. As the sociologist Ephraim Mizruchi puts it, the establishment of bohemia depends upon conditions where "status opportunities contract or organizations fail to expand in time to absorb" artistic producers (39). Under such conditions, artistic producers such as poets worked "to establish and monitor what they alone determined to be the highest standards of artistic output" (15). That is, artistic producers in bohemia start to set their own standards for what counts as good or meaningful work.

Gioia's notion that bohemia represented a market-driven world for poets is deeply at odds with the sociological consensus. In point of fact, bohemia represented a stage in literary development quite close to that which we have come to see in the (admittedly less colorful) world of MFA professionalization: in both cases, poetic value is determined by a community of poets and critics, not by a market. One could follow Mizruchi and argue that the development of writing programs is little more than organizations finally expanding to absorb the artistic producers they could not absorb during the time of literary bohemia. The absorption involved little change in the notion of the validating principle of poetry. In both conditions it remained a matter of autonomy, or poets deciding for themselves what was of value, and ignoring the market forces Gioia imagines were dominant in what he takes to have been happier times.

Like Gioia, Joseph Epstein laments the failure of contemporary poetry to be governed by market forces. "Sometimes it seems as if there isn't a poem written in this nation," he writes, "that isn't subsidized or underwritten by a grant either from a foundation or the government or a teaching salary or a fellowship of one kind or another" (Epstein). Unlike Gioia, he is too aware of the conditions and values of the pre-professionalized literary era he valorizes to claim that this was an era in which poets were broadly popular. Praising the modernists writing in the 1950s, Epstein tells us:

> They published their work in magazines read only by hundreds; their names were not known by most members of the educated classes; their following, such as it was, had a cultish character. But beyond this nothing else seems comparable [to the world of the writing programs]. Propel-

ling the modernist poets was a vision, and among some of them a
program—a belief that the nature of life had changed fundamentally
and that artists now had to change accordingly. . . . New, too, was their
attitude toward the reader, whom they, perhaps first among any writers
in history, chose in a radical way to disregard. They weren't out to *épater*.
If what they wrote was uncompromisingly difficult, they did not see this
as their problem. They wrote as they wrote. . . . Somehow, through the
quality of their writing, the authority of the sacrifices they made for
their art, the aura of adult seriousness conveyed in both work and life,
the modernist poets won through.

The "somehow" is, one fears, a little desperate. Epstein dearly wants
the poetry of the 1950s to have been central to the general culture of
the time, but he is too well-informed and intellectually honest to omit
mention of the evidence to the contrary. Unfortunately, he is not able
to prevent himself from simply dismissing it with a wave of the hand.

Should we wish to provide evidence for the centrality of poetry to
national culture in the 1950s, filling in the virtually blank space where
Epstein gives us a vague "somehow" and an even vaguer "won through,"
we would be a bit hard up. The only truly dramatic piece of evidence,
one oft-cited by critics and journalists, would be T. S. Eliot's appearance
before several thousand people in Minnesota. This event, prominently
misrepresented as a poetry reading in a baseball stadium in Peter Ackroyd's biography of Eliot, was in fact a lecture held in the rather smaller
confines of a university basketball arena. Few records of the event are
available, but those we have tend to deflate any sense that the event
represented anything like a massive popular interest in poetry in the
1950s. Consider the testimony of Theresa Enroth, an audience member
for Eliot's lecture, writing to the *New York Times* in 1995 to disabuse readers
of some inaccuracies in the paper's representation of the event:

> When Eliot appeared at the University of Minnesota in 1956, his perfor-
> mance had no similarity to what is generally meant by "poetry reading."
> He read his essay called "The Frontiers of Criticism." That the poet drew
> a big crowd probably had something to do with his having received the
> 1948 Nobel Prize in Literature.

For a great many readers at that time, his voice defined the disillusion-
ment and angst of the midcentury. In addition, Eliot's poetry and criticism

were central to the study of poetry in many college English departments where the New Criticism held dominion. The department lions at the University of Minnesota included, successively, Robert Penn Warren and Allen Tate. (Their friend John Crowe Ransom gave a poetry reading there—to a small crowd in the auditorium of the science museum.)

The cultural capital of the Nobel Prize, the novelty of the presence of a Nobel Laureate in a provincial city in the 1950s, and the incipient academicizing of poetry all seem to have played a role in the size of the audience, and the event was both atypical and unrepeatable, as the modesty of Ransom's audience shows. The notion that Eliot attracted an audience disillusioned with the dominant values of the times also argues against the idea that poetry was connected to the central values of our society in the 1950s.

When, then, was poetry popular, and in sympathy with the values of a broad public? When and where was it viable in terms of the values of the market? Epstein actually does give an example of such a time and place, before getting bogged down in nostalgia for the poetry of his own youth in the 50s. "The crowds in London once stood on their toes to see Tennyson pass;" writes Epstein, "today a figure like Tennyson probably would not write poetry and might not even read it. Poetry has been shifted—has shifted itself?—off center stage" (Epstein). To understand our own discursive condition, we need to contrast it not with the 1940s or 50s, but with the mid-Victorian period, when much poetry truly did have popular appeal, market viability, and a deep affinity with the values of the reading public. Only by such a contrast can we understand the forces that got us from there to here.

Empire of the Man of Letters

What, then, were the conditions capable of producing a crowd standing on tiptoe to see the poet Tennyson? The discursive situation of poetry—that is, the conditions of writing, publishing, and reception of the mid-Victorian period (roughly 1830 to 1870) differed sharply from those of our own time. The majority of verse published in journals appeared not in little magazines devoted solely, or even primarily, to poetry, but in more general journals, featuring poetry alongside essays, reviews, and reports of a kind we might not consider literary. This sort of publication, of course, is part of Barr, Gioia, and Epstein's imagined world of the modern poet before the professionalization of poetry. But what is important is not just the medium of publication (the general interest journal), but the way poetry was read when it appeared in those publications. Much more so than at any point in the twentieth century, poetry in the mid-Victorian period was read for reasons similar to the reasons the public read nonfiction prose. Indeed, the poet was not generally considered to be a writer categorically different from other kinds of writers: the poet was a subset of a much broader group, 'the men of letters,' a category now extinct. Historian T. W. Heyck describes the nature of the beast:

> By 'men of letters,' or 'literary men' the Victorians meant more than producers of literature as such. Towards the end of the century, it is true, 'men of letters' was beginning to take on the sense of its most common twentieth-century definition—a quaint, second-rate writer in *belles lettres*. But throughout most of the century, 'men of letters' was a broader and more respectable sobriquet, including a wide variety of writers—poets, novelists, biographers, historians, social critics, philosophers, and political economists. It was applied to writers of imaginative literature like Dickens, Thackeray, and Tennyson, to critics and social thinkers like Carlyle, Ruskin, and Arnold; and to political philosophers like Mill, G. H. Lewes, and John Morley. (24)

In our own world, the very existence of the professional journal called *Poets & Writers* asserts the deep division between poets and their relatively close cousins, fiction writers. We simply do not classify poets with historians, social critics, and writers of political economy, as the mid-Victorians did. We see poets as different from such writers, and we read them for different reasons than we read writers on economics. For the mid-Victorian, though, poets fit neatly into the broader category of the men of letters. Like others in the category, the poet wrote for the market, had work appear in general interest magazines and, most importantly, was read for the same reasons Ruskin, Thackeray, or Mill were read: for moral guidance.

The great majority of mid-Victorian readers came from the rising middle class that, in 1851, constituted some 20% of the population

(Cole 57). This class, growing into unprecedented political and social dominance in a rapidly changing and industrializing society, felt understandably dislocated. "As members of a relatively new social order," writes Heyck, "the middle class lacked the traditions and connections that might satisfy some of their needs, and they turned instead to publications for instruction and guidance." This need for guidance created a market for a certain kind of moralizing literature, and may even be credited with having "called into being the man of letters as a social type" (28). It was also responsible for raising the poet, as man of letters, to an unprecedented status and popularity. It is not for nothing that Carlyle titled two of his more famous lectures "The Hero as Man of Letters," and "The Hero as Poet." It speaks volumes about his audience's expectations, too, that they so heartily embraced Carlyle's claim that what England most needed was "a Prophet or Poet to teach us" (*On Heroes, Hero-Worship, and the Heroic in History* 8). To get a full sense of how closely the poet was associated with other kinds of writers, and how thoroughly didactic the role of the poet was in this high noon of the man of letters, we need look no further than the title of Alexander H. Japp's 1865 book *Three Great Teachers of Our Own Time: Carlyle, Tennyson and Ruskin,* although we might also do well to read a little of his text, especially his claim that he anticipates his readership as, in large measure, consisting of lovers of Tennyson "searching eagerly for truth, honestly inquiring what the great poet or rhythmic teacher of the age really means, and what his chief aims and ends are" (89). It's a notion of the poet entirely alien to our own. One can hardly imagine one of John Ashbery's readers calling him a "rhythmic teacher of the age" without tongue placed firmly in cheek.

Why, we should ask, would the middle class readership trust in poets to act as their moral teachers? To a great extent, this was because men of letters, including poets, were drawn from, and remained a part of, the same social class as the reading public, and as such they articulated that class's own views, anxieties, and values. Before the rise of mass literacy, the reading public had a tremendous social homogeneity—so much so that opinion in the public sphere of published writing was generally considered to be coterminous with the opinion of the middle class (Briggs 56–7). As Noel Annan has exhaustively documented, the men of letters came overwhelmingly from this class—and, indeed, the leading intellectual families of England frequently intermarried with the leading political and intellectual families of the dominant middle class. The men of letters were also in frequent face-to-face social contact with the leaders of the emerging political establishment. A partial list of the men of letters who rubbed shoulders with this establishment as members of the Athenaeum Club would include Matthew Arnold, Robert Browning, Edward Bulwer-Lytton, Thomas Carlyle, Arthur Hugh Clough, Charles Dickens, Thomas Hardy, Thomas Babington Macauley, John Ruskin, Robert Louis Stevenson, Alfred Lord Tennyson, William Makepeace Thackeray, Anthony Trollope, and many more. This was not an alienated group of intellectuals. Indeed, the self-interest of the men of letters was, before the migration of writers and thinkers into bohemia or academe, identical to the interest of the market-dependent middle class as a whole. While we have come to expect our poets to be in some (often vague) way oppositional to, or critical of, the dominant values of the middle class and the market in which that class makes its living, this was not the case in the mid-Victorian period. The man of letters spoke for, not against, the values of the broad reading public, a fact that lay behind the success of his works in the marketplace. As one Victorian reader, J. H. Froude, put it, when he and his peers read the poems of Tennyson "they became part of our minds, the expression, in exquisite language, of the feelings which were working in ourselves" (Cruse 187).

It is not the case, of course, that the Victorian poet, as man of letters, was limited to simple cheerleading for the expanding and expansionist middle class, with their ideals of patriotism, imperialism, deferred gratification, and duty—although a reader of "The Charge of the Light Brigade" may well be forgiven for thinking so. As the historian Stefan Collini has argued, the man of letters was at times expected to raise his voice in favor of mitigating the bad behavior of the dominant class. Such criticism did not, however, extend to criticizing the nature of the social and economic system itself: it was generally a matter of emphasizing the need of living up to one's personal ideals, and acting altruistically within the confines of the existing system (62–6). The moral guidance expected of the man of letters was not revolutionary or even oppositional: it was largely a matter of exhorting the reader to be a kinder version of the type of person he or she already was. One might think here of the critic Alan Sinfield's observation that Tennyson saw the poet's role as "recalling his society to its best self," not reforming it (176). Or one might think of Dickens' staggeringly popular *A Christmas Carol*, in which Ebenezer Scrooge never becomes a socialist: he merely becomes a more sensitive bourgeois.

Such were the discursive conditions under which the man of letters rose to prominence and established his imperium of letters. And here, in the mid-Victorian period rather than in the 1940s or 1950s, are the conditions for which writers like Gioia, Epstein, and Barr yearn: conditions in which poets are read widely, are taken seriously by the broad reading public, succeed in the marketplace, and are in conversation with other intellectuals. Though Barr and company don't know it, what they've really done is to mount a Victorian critique of contemporary poetry or, more properly, a Victorian critique of the discursive conditions of contemporary poetry (in fact, complaints such as theirs about poetic precocity and specialization had already begun to emerge at the end of the nineteenth century, perhaps most prominently in the writings of Frederic Harrison). What people like Barr, Gioia, and Epstein really yearn for is a return to the era when the poet functioned as a man of letters. Such an era was by no means the natural state of poetry, since there can be no such state. It was, instead, like our current situation, in that it was quite contingent on temporary circumstances. It was a brief zenith of popularity, in which the poet was no longer writing for a tiny audience while living on the patronage of the court or the church. The poet was not yet a bohemian, free but off in the margins of society; nor was the poet yet a professional, writing primarily for other professionals. How did the sun set on the poet's brief but ample empire? How, that is, did we get from there to here?

Twilight of the Man of Letters

A study of greater length than the present essay would, of course, be necessary to present anything like a full picture of the transformation of the world of the poet as man of letters into the world of the poet as creative writing professor. Two main forces can, nevertheless, be isolated here: changes in the nature of the reading public, and changes regarding the kind of the thinking that was considered useful in guiding the public. Both kinds of changes conspired to put an end to the relationship the poet had to the audience in the mid-Victorian period.

During the mid-Victorian apex of the man of letters, the poet tended to share a general outlook on the world with his readership. As members of the same class as their public (and, like that public, dependent on the forces of the market for their living) most poets shared an ideology with them. But this situation was dependent upon the small size and social exclusivity of the reading public. From the 1840s to 1900, literacy rates rose with unprecedented speed, and by 1900 illiteracy had been all but eliminated in England and Wales, with more than 97% of men and 96% of women in possession of at least basic reading skills (see Altick 188–213). One cannot decry such a development, but it did, in tandem with the rising financial wellbeing of the working classes, have the unfortunate effect of making the kind of publishing that had supported the poets and men of letters less profitable. Many of the newly literate lacked sufficient education to read or take an interest in the kind of work that had flourished during the noontime of the man of letters, and publishers found that the best return on their investments came from the publication of the kind of writing elite readers dismissed as the "penny-dreadful" novel, many of which sold in the range of sixty thousand copies, a figure almost no book of poetry could match. Poetry, which had for a time been a viable market commodity, began its long retreat to the realm of subsidized publishing.

Even among the more elite sort of readers, the affinity with poets and other men of letters began to fade. The rising middle class had turned to men of letters for guidance at a time when they were not yet confident in their status, and had not yet developed traditions and norms of conduct to sustain their sense of status. But as the nineteenth century wore on, the old, landed classes increasingly intermarried with the bourgeoisie, forming a newly confident class that developed an ethos of self-interest, utilitarianism, and conspicuous material consumption—an ethos that represented a rejection of the moralizing of the men of letters (Heyck 198). Not only had poetry become less viable in the expanded book market:

it had become less interesting to the class that once turned to it for guidance. The bourgeoisie, no longer lacking confidence about its utilitarian and materialist tendencies, broke with the poets. They were decreasingly in need of buying what the mid-Victorian poets were selling.

Reinforcing this turn away from the poet as moralist were revolutions in the realm of knowledge. While the public had once looked on the man of letters as a source of truth, the growth of science and of all forms of quantifiable knowledge reduced the status of the poet. Few among the mid-Victorian men of letters saw this, although Carlyle did, writing prophetically as early as 1829 that the sciences were "engrossing every day more respect and attention" and that soon the public would assume that "what cannot be investigated and understood mechanically, cannot be investigated and understood at all" ("Signs of the Times"). The situation had become much clearer for writers working in the later decades of the century, though. Social reformer Beatrice Webb, for example, looked back on the later Victorian years and asked:

> Who will deny that the men of science were the leading British intellectuals of the period? That it was they who stood out as men of genius with international reputations; that it was they who were the self confident militants of the period; that it was they who were routing the theologians, confounding the mystics, imposing their theories on the philosophers, their inventions on the capitalists, and their discoveries on medical men; whilst they were at the same time snubbing the artists, ignoring the poets . . . (126–7)

Even that greatest of the men of letters, Matthew Arnold, wondered if the time for his kind was passing, writing in 1882, "the question is raised whether, to meet the needs of modern life, the predominance ought not now to pass from letters to science." Perhaps most telling about the decline of the status of poetry as a guide to truth and morals are the comments of the ever-pessimistic Thomas Hardy who, after courting public scandal in his prose works, wrote in 1897:

> Perhaps I can express more fully in verse ideas and emotions which run counter to the inert crystallized opinion—hard as rock—which the vast body of men have vested interests in supporting. . . . If Galileo had said in verse that the world moved, the Inquisition might have left him alone. (284–5)

Of course Hardy was wrong about the Inquisition: heresy in verse or prose amounted to the same thing in Galileo's time. But the point Hardy makes about his own time is clear. Poetry was no longer considered a guide to life by the broad reading public, so controversial claims made in poetry lost their capacity to provoke much response.

The rise of science as a source of truth was, to a large degree, the product of the professionalization of science. Early in the nineteenth century science was conducted either on an amateur basis, or as an adjunct to profit-oriented industrial research. Over the course of the century it took on something approaching its modern form as a profession, something autonomous from the immediate concerns of industry and the market. It entered the university and, in the process, changed the ancient academic institutions, remaking them along the lines of professionalized research and autonomous fields of study. This, too, had an effect on poetry, taking it closer to the world of the poetry professional. Literature entered the university and became a professional field of study. Literary academics did not write for the market, nor did they share in the market-based form of life of the middle class at large, so their experiences and values were not, by and large, in accord with those of the business-based middle class. They shied away from both moralism and the idea of utility. Walter Pater, for example, ensconced in Oxford, wrote in favor of literature as an opportunity for nothing more than intensity of experience. For this he was pilloried by the bourgeois press. One anonymous critic, writing for *Blackwood's*, saw Pater as belonging to "a class removed from ordinary mankind by that ultra-culture and academical contemplation of the world as a place chiefly occupied by other beings equally cultured and refined," a group that "forms an inner circle of illuminati in almost every university" (604). Clearly the Paterian idea of literature did not please the middle class readership. It did, however, inspire Oscar Wilde and an entire generation of poets in the aesthetic movement. Many of these figures, driven from the marketplace by developments in mass literacy and publishing, took to bohemia, where the idea of poetry for itself, or at any rate for other poets, took root in fertile ground.

Professionalized literary studies and bohemianized poetry were close cousins, both products of broad shifts in economics and culture that took poetry and the broad reading public in different directions. The wonder isn't that poetry writing became a professionalized academic career, then: the real wonder is that it took so long, since by the end of the nineteenth century the man of letters had become all but extinct and his role had, in the words of T. W. Heyck, "altered from cultural leadership to one of isolated practice of an art—from a concept of a cultured minority integrated with the whole of society to one of a minority culture" (190).

Bleeding Poets with Leeches

For the world of the men of letters to have endured, so too would the conditions that existed before the rise of mass literacy, before the rise of science, before the establishment of middle-class self-confidence, and before the conversion of academe from a training center for clergy to a modern center of professional knowledge. It is by no means clear that return to such conditions would be worth the price, even if it were possible to destroy working-class literacy, intimidate the middle class with aristocratic arrogance, discredit science, and disestablish the universities except for the departments of classics and theology. No one advocates such draconian actions, though, perhaps because most critics who yearn for the discursive situation native to the mid-Victorian period imagine that discursive situation to have occurred later, in the 1940s and 50s. What, in the absence of a return to mid-Victorian conditions, do they offer to remedy what they consider to be the benighted current condition of poetry? Would their remedies, if put into effect, produce results? The remedies can be broken into two broad categories: market-based solutions and cultural paternalism. Neither, when looked at in the context of available evidence, would appreciably change the conditions of contemporary poetry. Decades of complaint have, it turns out, given us remedies about as efficacious as the bleeding of poets with leeches.

Thomas Disch advocates the most extreme form of market solution. Seeing the writing programs as a form of subsidization for an otherwise unviable poetic commodity, Disch calls for "the disestablishment of poetry workshops as an academic institution" (14), although how the removal of such programs—with so many vested interests—would be accomplished is left unsaid. The question of whether the solution would work in bringing poetry back to a broad audience is also left unaddressed. Given that the public, for complex historical reasons, no longer demands poetry as it did in the mid-Victorian period, one rather doubts that a mere ending of subsidy would return poetry to prominence. Given, too, the changes in the size and composition of the reading public since the mid-Victorian period, one does not see a return of poetry to viability as a marketable commodity. In the end, what Disch offers is less a plan than a statement of resentment for subsidized writing, made, it is worth noting, by a man who makes his living as a science fiction writer—that is, as a writer who needs to succeed in the marketplace. His solution is less a solution *per se* than it is a version of the private sector's resentment of the very existence of the public sector.

John Barr is less extreme in his views, but like Disch he sees the market as the solution to poetry's lack of prominence. He sees poetry as deeply subsidized, saying that poets "are sustained by a system of fellowships, grants, and other subsidies that absolve recipients of the responsibility to write books that a reader who is not a specialist might enjoy, might even buy." He does not call for changes in the audience, saying that "the responsibilities of the public to poetry are nil." His primary suggestion is to change the product to make it more appealing to the consuming public. Significantly, what he advocates is a return to large-scale poetry of "moral urgency" that can "instruct through pleasing." That is, he wants a poetry of moral guidance, of the kind that appealed to the mid-Victorian reader. What he does not apprehend is that the conditions that made a broad reading public yearn for such a poetry no longer apply.[1] Of course Barr is a product of the market-

---

1. Indeed, Barr's own long, morally uplifting book of poetry, *Grace*, published by a non-academic press, hovers somewhat below the abysmal position of my own, amoral, non-uplifting book of poems—written largely during a professor's summers, therefore subsidized—in online sales rankings. At the time of writing, my book *Home and Variations* was the 2,262,913th most popular book on Amazon, while Barr's was the 2,641,383rd most popular. Both books have been out for some years, and neither Barr nor I seem to be succeeding in the marketplace, with or without subsidy, with or without moral uplift. It is with some small and illegitimate pleasure that I notice used copies of his book sell for one cent in the marketplace, a mere 1/79th the price of a used copy of *Home and Variations*. In this one limited sense my subsidized amorality has, it seems, a stronger market than Barr's attempt at a market-based moralism.

oriented world, having spent much of his career working with such energy trading companies as Dynegy and Enron, so it is perhaps unsurprising to see a certain market fundamentalism on his part ("the human mind," Barr claims, "is a marketplace"). But the particular market-based reforms he proposes for poetry don't take full account of the nature of the current potential market for poetry (Barr).

Dana Gioia, whose career has involved both high-ranking corporate positions and, more recently, sector administration, offers a mixed-bag of market-based and public-sector solutions to the problem of poetry's lack of popularity. Much of what he suggests are versions of cross-marketing, of putting poetry in front of readers who don't seek it out on their own. Poetry readings, he suggests, should "mix poetry with the other arts, especially music," a strategy intended to draw fans of other arts into the proximity of poets and poems (22). Poets should, too, "recapture the attention of the broader intellectual community by writing for non-specialist publications" (23). Assuming editors would comply, this would also put poetry in front of audiences who don't generally seek it out, potentially converting these readers into a large fan base for poetry.

Gioia combines these market-based ideas with a kind of cultural paternalism, a paternalism he shares with another nonprofit sector employee, Charles Bernstein. Both suggest using public radio to put poetry in front of millions of potential poetry readers (Gioia 23, Bernstein). This isn't a matter of responding to public demand, as the putting of poetry on commercial radio would have to be. Instead, it is in the long tradition of paternalism in public media, which assumes that (to quote the first General Director of BBC radio, Sir John Reith) "an active faith that a supply of good things will create a demand for them" and assumes, too, that we who know what those good things are should not wait "for the demand to express itself" (see Barnow 247–8).

The problem with both cross-marketing and the Reithian use of the public media is that believing either would do much to change the rate of poetry reading flies in the face of the data collected by the National Opinion Research Center. According to the 2006 N.O.R.C. report *Poetry in America*, even people who "read and like the poetry that they find in unexpected places" say "it doesn't inspire them to seek out more poetry" (iv). While John Barr (who heads the organization that commissioned the study) is technically right in saying the study indicates that when people find poems in public transportation and general interest magazines, they will often "read it when they see it" (or, the case of radio, listen when they hear it) (Barr), this statement blithely elides the survey's finding that "incidental exposure seems to reinforce existing poetry behaviors" (69) of reading or not-reading verse, and that such exposure has no effect on influencing people's "intent to read poetry in the future" (71). It is as if people saw advertisements, but were not influenced by them. This can hardly be considered a successful strategy for increasing poetry's readership. One wonders how John Barr, whose foundation spent more than $700,000 on the report, could omit mention of such a pessimistic finding, although perhaps the answer is in the question itself.

Underdevelopment and the Last Professors

Short of a return to the social conditions of the mid-Victorian era, can there be a return to a discursive situation in which poetry matters to a broad public? One hopes not. When we consider the evidence, we find that, historically, the conditions under which poetry becomes widely popular are not conditions we should seek out. In addition to the singular mid-Victorian situation, we find poetry to be prominent in another kind of situation. Sadly, though, this is a situation of socio-political disenfranchisement. The great scholar of Irish literature Declan Kiberd explains:

> A writer in a free state works with the easy assurance that literature is but one of the social institutions to project the values which the nation admires, others being the law, the government, the army, and so on. A writer in a colony knows that these values can be fully embodied only in the written word: hence the daunting seriousness with which literature is taken by subject peoples. This almost prophetic role of the artist is often linked to 'underdeveloped' societies. (118)

In colonies, and among people oppressed by their governments and unable to find expression in the institutional life of their countries, poetry takes on a great social importance. But just as we would not wish to return to mid-Victorian levels of literacy and social development just to see the rise of a new Tennyson, we would not wish to fall victim to colonization just to have our own Celtic Revival. Those of us who live with discursive conditions that keep poetry unpopular may count ourselves lucky.

None of this is to say that the present professionalized conditions will continue. Just as the poet as man of letters depended on specific historical contingencies, so too is the idea of the poet as a professional working in relative autonomy from the market. The oversupply of academically credentialed poets points toward a shifting of the center of gravity away from academe. Moreover, academe itself is facing increasing pressure to respond to the forces of the market. In Britain, this includes new government guidelines for departments to demonstrate the market utility of their activities. In the United States the situation remains milder, but, as Frank Donoghue argues in *The Last Professors: The Corporate University and the Fate of the Humanities*, the encroachment of market values on the previously semi-autonomous academic system is well under way, and is probably irreversible. Critics who long for changes in the relation of poets to the public and the market may take comfort in knowing that some sort of change is surely underway, although it will occur with or without any of the efforts at publicity and cross-marketing those critics may make.

Works Cited

Ackroyd, Peter. *T. S. Eliot: A Life*. New York: Simon and Schuster,1985. Print.
Altick, Richard. *The English Common Reader: A Social History of the Mass Reading Public, 1800-1900*. 2nd ed. Columbus: Ohio State UP, 1998. Print.
Annan, Noel. "The Intellectual Aristocracy." *Studies in Social History*. Ed. J. H. Plumb. London: Longmans, 1955. 241-87. Print.
Anonymous. "New Books." *Blackwood's* November (1873): 604. Print.
Arnold, Matthew. *Literature and Science*. Lancashire, n.d. Web.
Bain, Marc. "The End of Verse?" *Newsweek* web exclusive, March 25, 2009. Web.
Barouw, Erik. *A Tower in Babel: A History of Broadcasting in the United States*, vol.1. New York: Oxford UP, 1966. Print.
Barr, John. "American Poetry in the New Century." *Poetry Foundation*. 23 October 2006. Web.
Bawer, Bruce. *Prophets and Professors*. Brownsville, Oregon: Storyline, 1995. Print.
Beach, Christopher. *Poetic Culture: Contemporary American Poetry Between Community and Institution*. Evanston: Northwestern UP, 1999. Print.

Bernstein, Charles. "Warning—Poetry Area: Publics Under Construction." *Electronic Poetry Center*. 25 November 1996. Web.

Bourdieu, Pierre. *The Field of Cultural Production: Essays on Art and Literature.* Ed. Randal Johnson. Cambridge: Polity, 1993. Print.

Briggs, Asa. "The Language of Class in Early Nineteenth-Century England." *Essays in Labor History.* Ed. Asa Briggs and John Saville. London: MacMillan, 1960: 43-73. Print.

Carlyle, Thomas. *On Heroes, Hero-Worship, and the Heroic in History.* New York: Wiley, 1861. Print.

Carlyle, Thomas. "Signs of the Times." *The Victorian Web,* 2007. Web.

Cole, G. D. H. *Studies in Class Structure.* London: Routledge, 2003. Print.

Collini, Stefan. *Public Moralists: Political Thought and Intellectual Life in Britain 1850-1930.* Oxford: Oxford UP, 1991. Print.

Cruse, Amy. *Victorians and Their Books.* London: Allen, 1962. Print.

Disch, Thomas. *The Castle of Indolence.* New York: Picador, 1995. Print.

Donoghue, Frank. *The Last Professors: The Corporate University and the Fate of the Humanities.* New York: Fordham UP, 2008. Print.

Enroth, Theresa. Letter to *New York Times,* April 23, 1995: 735. Print.

Epstein, Joseph. "Who Killed Poetry?" *Commentary Magazine.* August 1988. Web.

Graña, Cesar. *Bohemian vs. Bourgeois.* New York: Basic, 1964. Print.

Hall, Donald. "Poetry and Ambition." *Academy of American Poets. N.d.* Web.

Hardy, Thomas. *The Life of Thomas Hardy.* London: Macmillan, 1962. Print.

Harrison, Frederic. *Autobiographic Memoirs,* vol. 1. London: MacMillan, 1911. Print.

Heyck, T. W. *The Transformation of Intellectual Life in Victorian England.* Chicago: Lyceum, 1982. Print.

Japp, Alexander H. *Three Great Teachers of Our Own Time: Carlyle, Tennyson And Ruskin.* London: Smith, 1865. Print.

Mizruchi, Ephraim. "Bohemia as a Means of Social Regulation." *On Bohemia: The Code of the Self-Exiled.* Eds. Cesar and Marigay Graña. New Jersey: Transaction, 1990: 1-41. Print.

Nester, Daniel. "Goodbye to All Them." *Morning News.* 23 September 2009. Web.

Nester, Daniel. "An Interview with Daniel Nester." *Bookslut.* January 2010. Web.

Parry, Albert. *Garrets and Pretenders.* New York: Dover, 1960. Print.

Shetley, Vernon. *After the Death of Poetry: Poet and Audience in Contemporary America.* Durham: Duke UP, 1993. Print.

Schwartz, Lisa K., Lisbeth Goble, Ned English and Robert F. Bailey. *Poetry in America: Review of the Findings.* Chicago: National Opinion Research Center, 2006. Print.

Sinfield, Alan. *Alfred Tennyson.* Oxford: Blackwell, 1986. Print.

Webb, Beatrice. *My Apprenticeship.* London: Longmans, 1926. Print.

The Moves:
Common Maneuvers in Contemporary Poetry

Elisa Gabbert

Poetry is kind of like chess—there are an infinite number of possible games, but each game tends to be made up of certain
recognizable moves. Experienced chess players know the classic
openings and the classic defenses, along with their sexy names (the
Catalan System, the Two Knights Defense, the Queen's Gambit Declined).
In chess, familiarity, and proficiency, with established moves is not a
weakness but a strength—even a given.

The longer one lives as a "practicing poet," the easier it becomes to
recognize techniques, devices, and strategies as patterns—as common,
abstracted moves. You can see this as a cynical or overly analytical way
of reading, but it feels inevitable, as one both reads and writes more
poetry, to become aware of the seams, to realize not everything is original and born of pure inspiration. At this stage of poethood, some of
the innocence and awe of reading are gone, but with this process comes
greater understanding.

It can be valuable to know your own moves—your go-to tricks and
turns and images—as a defense against overusing or misusing them,
against writing formulaic poetry. As a reader, it's valuable to know a

particular poet's signature moves, as well as what moves are popular in a given cohort or school, and over a given time period, in order to speak convincingly and compellingly about style and trends.

But moves aren't just something to be identified and then avoided. There's no chess—and no dancing—without moves. If each of a poet's poems were unlike the others in every way, there would be no reason to prefer some poets to others; one could only have favorite poems, not favorite poets. A move is just a small element of a poet's larger style, and having a few distinctive moves, or maneuvers that can be isolated and imitated, is a mark of having a strong and recognizable voice.

What follows is a list of common moves I have identified in contemporary poetry. Lest this exercise seem condescending, let it be known that I am guilty of committing a great many of these moves, but choose examples from my peers, heroes, and enemies rather than my own work where possible.

Exposed Revision

For example, from Alice Fulton's "About Face":

At least embarrassment is not an imitation.
It's intimacy for beginners,
the orgasm no one cares to fake.
I almost admire it. I almost wrote despise.

Exposed Revision is the poetry equivalent of a play that breaks the fourth wall. In this maneuver, the poet reveals a backtracking, a change of mind or a change of heart, and documents the change, as though via Microsoft Word's Track Changes feature, rather than concealing it. As such the reader becomes aware of the author *qua author*, or the speaker as a facet of the author; the process of writing and rewriting is foregrounded rather than disguised. A popular variation of this move is revision by way of the phrase "I mean," as in "Confession" by Suzanne Wise:

I can only imagine
how hard it must be for you
to believe me. I mean, to hold
blame. I mean, to be you.

In order to succeed, Exposed Revision should revise an idea rather than merely alter the wording. In an advanced example ("Little Happier" by Justin Marks), the idea in question appears in the first stanza:

> All that whiteness was still before me,
> a field of snow on which
> not one foot seemed to have left a print.
> Around the field, cold and rickety trees,
> their shadows hovering
> as if they were not shadows but shade,
> independent of what cast their image
> on the ground. It was as if
> there were no tree . . . whiteness without end,
> but touched with such shading as needed
> to keep things interesting.

This idea is not revised until the final line, some thirty lines later: "how naïve I was to say, / *whiteness without end.*"

The X of Y Construction

The X of Y Construction has been in use for centuries, and its popularity persists to this day. This syntactical construction has the effect of making any two-word phrase seem automatically more poetic: Witness "light box" versus "box of light," "time slot" versus "slot of time," "pink grapefruit" versus "grapefruit of pink." Because it is so easy to apply and so effective, it is easy to overuse. Take "Whether" by Lisa Russ Spaar (boldface mine):

> Out of a cinched **sack of bones**, the dog's half-cast
> opiate eyes ask *can't you hear the moths, pelting*
>
> *the pear glass?* & then there is nothing else I can hear,
> bulbs opal and ignited as felted **anus-stars**
>
> **of snow** spot the porch, blast the poplars:
> the thumbscrew aortal **pulse of Philomela.**
>
> *Whose fork is this?* my mother asked me, pointing to her cane
> in the **dark of the backseat** last week. I was driving.
>
> *Probably one of the kids'* I replied, *they're always trashing*
> *my car*, but truly they are the brilliant **canto of my antiquity.**
>
> I search her eyes, terrified for **signs of pain.**
> She is light, and waits not for the **flip of a switch.**

Nor is my love portable, quick lick in the **history of the world**.
For her, do I get down. For her, my fork and cane.

Here the X of Y Construction is reduced to a tic. But like any move,
it can be done well, when done with restraint, as in "The Sidewalk" by
Jessica Fjeld: "Only when the five-and-dime / shutters up beneath a fall
of ash and maidenhair / will anyone give voice to vice."

Abstract Epistolary

The Abstract Epistolary—the word "Dear" preceding an abstract
noun, inanimate object, or some other entity or part of speech other
than a person, the usual subject of epistolary address—may occur in the
title, in the first line, mid-poem, or in some combination thereof. See
"Dear Final Journey," by Lynn Emanuel:

> Dear Noose, Dear Necktie, Dear Cravat,
> Salutations, big ship, toiling the dark waters
> Of death. Dear Freighter, in whose hold the oily links
> Of the anchor's chain, like snakes, are coiled. Dear Oily
> Waters, salve and balm, black disk of ocean across which,
> Dark Craft, you creak, loom, until your black gobbles
> The horizon up. Dear black firmament and earth,
> Ditch of the kicked in. World shut and over,
> Mingy and dim. Dear Line, Dear Sinker,
> Noose and Hook,

Hello.

This move creates the impression of a poet both introspective and
extremely sensitive to all manners of being, not just people, mammals, and
the environment. It is so of-the-moment, so overused as to become tiresome
and finally appalling, in the manner of number one pop songs. Anyone still
actively practicing the Abstract Epistolary should be gently but firmly rep-
rimanded. This move may be used again ironically in ten or more years.

Verbing the Noun

Verbing the Noun is an intermediate maneuver—not overly difficult
to achieve, but not so simple as to invite rampant abuse. It has a renew-
able power to delight. Examples include: "perceiving only how vertigo

/ secretaries me into the office" (from *Scape* by Joshua Harmon); "As certain and invisible as / Red scarves silking endlessly // From a magician's hollow hat" (from "The Halo That Would Not Light" by Lucie Brock-Broido); and "little reindeers / hoofing murderously" (from "[when you touch down upon this earth. little reindeers]" by D. A. Powell). The risk, especially apparent in the third example, is a sort of precious cutesiness; it can also seem show-offy, but then, many moves carry this risk. Note that other parts of speech can be verbed, and verbs can be nouned (as in "a lynch / of light" from "How Can It Be I Am No Longer I" also by Brock-Broido), though this practice is less common.

Comparing Something to Itself

Comparing Something to Itself is a somewhat cynical move. See "At Peter Pan Mini Golf After the Wedding of Rebecca and Brian, or Any Binary System" by Dan Boehl:

> I could say this guy was like Spicoli,
> or I could say this guy was like Sean Penn,
> and both would be wrong because really
> this guy is like a guy that works weekends
> for the family mini-golf business.

See also Heather Christle's "The Handsome Man": "My god you were beautiful, / your sword sticking out like a sword." The move is cynical in that it exhibits a fed-up-ness with similes, and by extension poetic tropes in general, as though to say, "Why compare? Why evoke via metaphor what I could tell you directly?" In its rejection of the simile, so classical a device one hardly registers it as a move anymore, Comparing Something to Itself is almost an anti-move, and certainly references anti-poetry.[1]

The Self-Aware Poem

The Self-Aware Poem is a poem that makes explicit reference to poetry and especially to itself, as a poem. For example: "The Vandals" by Alan Michael Parker begins with the lines: "In the poem about the vandals, the vandals / Back their Dodge 4 x 4 up to the door." This poem *is* the poem

---

1. See Nicanor Parra (*Poems and Anti-Poems*) and the ensuing tradition—basically, poems that break away from poetic convention.

about the vandals, natch. Or from "XX" by Sampson Starkweather: "I suffer. Is that okay to say? I was talking / to the poem ANYWAY." Self-reference, often ironic, and meta-poetry are very much a product of postmodernism. Like Exposed Revision, the Self-Aware Poem calls attention to its artifice, and is therefore as much about form as content. If, as critic Terry Barrett claims, "All art is in part about other art," the Self-Aware Poem simply makes this *aboutness* explicit. However, some readers may feel that such references to poetry are redundant (much as Roger Ebert dismisses 3-D movies on the basis that conventional film is "already in 3-D as far as your mind is concerned": "When you see Lawrence of Arabia growing from a speck as he rides toward you across the desert, are you thinking, 'Look how slowly he grows against the horizon'? Our minds use the principle of perspective to provide the third dimension. Adding one artificially can make the illusion less convincing.").

Extreme Egotism

Like so many contemporary moves, Extreme Egotism is a loud form of irony. It posits a laughably self-important speaker, as in "My Ravine" by Dan Chiasson: "How will you know what my poem is like / until you've gone down my ravine" (overuse of the personal pronouns "I," "me," and "my" are often indicative of Extreme Egotism, but such overuse isn't sufficient; the overuse must be intentional). Similarly, in Chiasson's "Vermont": "I was the west / once. I was paradise." Another example can be found in the chapbook *Why I Am White* by Mathias Svalina: "I wasn't going to tell you about my boats, / but now I want to tell you about my boats." Extreme Egotism usually seems to hold a specific group or person up for ridicule (e.g., wealthy white men).

Facts and Figures

Facts and Figures[2] are used to give a poem a faux-scientific air. For example: Ben Lerner's "Mad Lib Elegy," which includes a string of Facts and Figures: "Migrant workers spend 23 hours a day / removing tiny

---

2. Thanks to Steven D. Schroeder, who identified this move on his blog (http://steve-schroeder.info/blog/).

seeds from mixtures / they cannot afford to smoke / and cannot afford not to smoke"; "70% of pound animals will be euthanized. / 94% of pound animals would be euthanized / if given the choice"; and finally:

> There are two kinds of people in the world
> those that condemn parking lots as monstrosities,
> 'the ruines of a broken World,' and those
> that respond to their majesty emotionally.
> 70% of the planet is covered in parking lots.
> 94% of a man's body is parking lot.

Another example is Danielle Aquiline's "Autobiogeography":

> Fact: Maps are only 87% accurate.
> Also fact: I am approximately 87% ocean.
> Depending on how you look at it,
> we are either surrounded by water, or water
> is completely surrounded by us.

Facts and Figures need not be accurate or true, and in fact they are usually quite evidently false, sardonically calling attention to the tendency of statistics to be biased, selective, or otherwise manipulated and manipulative. Facts and Figures also call attention to the tendency for readers to assume that poetic lines have truth value—that events depicted in narrative poems are "based on a true story," and that the speaker of a poem is identical to the author.

Mention of a Forest Animal

In poetry, as in band names and hipster design, forest animals are a trendy accent. Poems in which an animal is a primary figure (i.e., in which the animal could not be excised without seriously altering the poem), such as William Stafford's "Traveling Through the Dark" and other roadkill poems, or Wallace Stevens's "A Rabbit as King of the Ghosts," do not count; this move constitutes a glancing mention, as though the animals were dabbed into the background of a landscape as an afterthought. Including a deer, a rabbit, an owl, or a wolf in a poem that isn't otherwise indicative of nature poetry serves to make the poet appear spiritual in a relaxed way. For example: from "Only So Much Fits in a Petri Dish" by Julia Cohen and Mathias Svalina:

When the tree climbs down its bark, I follow
seedlings buried in cake. I've hidden the sin in roofing,
de-veined by a plum falling from the child's hand.

A wolf of her own.

Animals remind us of all that is cute, beautiful, and terrifying in the world; they add a nod to the sublime with minimal risk of looking boring or religious.

The Casual Hedge

Another anti-poem move, the Casual Hedge is a rejection of the elevated speech and carefully plotted rhetoric of capital-P Poetry from eras past. For example: "I'm sort of in a dunebuggy" (from "Kasmir" by Jon Leon). In addition to "sort of," "kind of" or "kinda," the suffix "-ish," and the estimative use of "like" (as in "My sister & I once spent the day / walking around in Brooklyn. / We watched a capybara do nothing, for like an hour" from "Contrast Girls" by Shanna Compton) constitute a partial list of Casual Hedges. This and other anti-moves are on the "cool" end of the continuum, if we plot moves on a scale from cold to hot, in that they cause the poem to appear effortless or easily written. More artful or writerly "warm" moves (such as allusions and extended metaphors), from the perspective of a "cool" poet, may cause poems to appear to be "trying too hard." But for the purposes of this exercise, apparent lack of exertion is nonetheless a move.

Poetic Allusion as Joke

The Poetic Allusion as Joke is lukewarm or perhaps lukecool on the aforementioned scale—an allusion implies effort and learnedness, but both are undermined when the objective is humor. For example: From "As If to Say" by Chris Nealon: "I seriously have a mind of winter." This is a variation on the strategy (usually poem-wide rather than identifiable to a single move) of mixing high and low diction, perhaps most famously embraced by John Ashbery. Diction mixing is an excellent way to add texture to a poem, but the Poetic Allusion as Joke does run the risk of seeming snide or disrespectful toward the alluded to.

The Throwaway Pun

The Throwaway Pun can be distinguished from a pun proper by intention and context. Similar to the Poetic Allusion as Joke, the Throwaway Pun tries to "have it both ways." It's an overtly authored joke that seems to apologize for itself or admit its own limits (outside the context of, say, a limerick, a pun is a cheap kind of humor). Take the following line from "Play it Again, Salmonella" by Jeffrey McDaniel: "I'm a card-carrying member of a canceled party." Even the title seems to come equipped with built-in groans. Another: "ACTUALLY *SAY* LA VIE" from Karl Parker's "Horn o' Plenty." This move is borrowed directly from the school of American comedy that celebrates bad jokes as good jokes as long as they are told with awareness. This is a variety of camp.

The Revised Cliché

Closely related to the Poetic Allusion as Joke, the Revised Cliché is an intentional misquote (but of a common phrase, rather than a well-known line) used with an eye toward humor, surprise, and the comfortable novelty of the varied familiar. Karl Parker's "Autobiographia" employs two in a row: "life is scared. Dogs only rarely eat other dogs." Like the Throwaway Pun, the Revised Cliché can convey ironic self-deprecation, by suggesting fallibility along with awareness of that fallibility—it indicates a willingness to be wrong, but not without purpose. Unfortunately, the more interesting the revision, the more this move risks feeling "too clever by half," and readers may question why the poet cannot be profound with scaffolding.

Fill in the Blank

Fill in the Blank is an auto-erasure. This move employs a literal blank space or otherwise asks the reader to do the work of completing a line. Ben Lerner's "Mad Lib Elegy" (quoted in "Facts and Figures" above) ends each stanza with Fill in the Blank:

> Finish your children. Adopt an injury.
>   'I'm going to my car. When I get back,
>   I'm shooting everybody.'
>   [line omitted in memory of_____]

This is actually a double application of the move, since in addition to the blank provided for a departed person or thing of your choosing, Lerner claims that the "real" closing line of each stanza has been removed. Fill in the Blank may also take the form of a note to self—in other words, the poet seems to have made a note to fill in a blank with a good or better word, phrase, image, metaphor, or other device, but then chooses to preserve the note in lieu of the planned replacement text. This, of course, is another cool move; it says, "I'm not going to break a sweat over this." Ana Božičević uses this variation of Fill in the Blank in "God Is President, She's the Rose of the World": "And the edges of objects: wavy / in the eye that's about to cry, // a twitter running down the spine of. . . / Oh God, it can't be. (Insert song of mourning.)" Another variation is filler words, as in "*God and time, spine of the world*—yawn, blah, blah, schma. . ." (from the same poem); also, in "Ode to Cotton": "While nautilus motions / sketch an inside future all over the something-something." Filler words serve the same note-to-self purpose as Fill in the Blank but are borderline onomatopoeic, suggesting the word on the tip of the tongue.

Intentional Ambiguity

Intentional Ambiguity is another product of postmodernist/deconstructionist criticism (i.e., the reader's interpretation is as valid as the author's intention; neither has primacy). Take, for example, the phrase "I run a toy glue factory" from "I Had My Headphones On" by Karl Parker. This could be interpreted in at least three ways: 1) I run a factory that makes glue used in toys. 2) I run a factory that makes toy-sized or pretend glue. 3) I run a glue factory that is itself toy-sized or pretend. In the unreal, or nightmare-real, world of the poem, these options seem equally likely. By withholding any disambiguating signs or information, the poet suggests that such "facts" have no consequence, and that poems do not traffic in facts in any case. In a way, Intentional Ambiguity is related to the unreliable narrator of fiction.

Scare Quotes

In poetry or otherwise, Scare Quotes—quotation marks used around text that is not a direct quote—can signify a number of things. Primarily, usages fall into one of three categories:

- The author is distancing herself from the word(s) in question
- The author is using the word(s) sarcastically or ironically
- The author is using the word(s) metaphorically (in the "if you will" sense)

It is also possible that the quotation marks themselves are being used ironically, to mock the inappropriate use or overuse of Scare Quotes. Scare Quotes have recently become associated with the Tao Lin school of ironic detachment, but it is often difficult to distinguish between Scare Quotes used in the manner of Tao Lin and Scare Quotes used in critique or mockery of Tao Lin. Indeed, it is not clear that there is any difference. This example from Lin's "an easy way to eat a lot of calories is to eat a block of cheese" may illustrate the point:

> something happened around 2 p.m. and i felt really bad
> i began 'an extremely vague, kind of funny' process to make myself
>   feel better
> near 14th street and 3rd avenue i felt that i was 'failing' 'a lot'

Perhaps a more traditional example of distancing via Scare Quotes can be found in "Let's Say" by Bob Perelman: "A page is being beaten / back across the face of 'things.'"

The Caps Lock Key

Poets use the Caps Lock Key to render part of a poem, or even an entire poem, in all capital letters. On the Internet, writing in all caps is usually interpreted as "shouting." In the context of a poem, however, the Caps Lock Key can have quite different effects. It may give the poem the feel of a telegram, imbuing the words with a flat, affectless tone, free of the anger of shouting. The lines may also seem mechanical, as though scrolling by on ticker tape or arriving by machine print-out; transcribed in real time as though by dictation; or translated in real time as though via a medium (a Ouija board has only capital letters). "Even As We Speak" by Ben Mazer is a full-poem example of the Caps Lock Key; the following is an excerpt:

> ORPHANS. POPPY. MISTAKEN IDENTITY. LIGHT IN THE
> HALLWAY. ROSES OF DAWNING OVER THE SHOULDER.
> POE. POE. NOT EVEN DARKNESS. NEVER GIVE A SUCKER
> AN EVEN BREAK. AND THERE IS NO TIME, NO TIME. NO.

WITH THE CAT HOWLING TO BE LET IN. NO NEED TO
WRITE. ONLY THIS WHAT I'M TELLING YOU. TELLING
MYSELF. THERE IS A BEGINNING TO ALL THIS. AN
OCCASION. SCOTTISH BAGPIPES ARE ITS EQUIVALENT,
BUT IT BEAMS DOWN IN SPECKLED LIGHTS. SPOKEN
LIGHTS. I WOULDN'T SAY. GOAT LIGHT. SAWDUST.

The fifth section of Ana Božičević's "Some Occurrences on the 7:18
to Penn" is all in caps except for the first line:

And the stars go:

THINGS ARE NOT LOOKING GOOD FOR US
MOLESTED BY HAIRCUTS ON LAW AND ORDER AND WHATS
    GONE WRONG
WITH THE SKYLINE, WHY,
INSTEAD OF READING A BOOK YOU READ STAR OR THE
    TOOTHPASTE, LOST IN AN ANCIENT ALMANAC

ANNE CARSON IN HEAVEN NERVOUS DESPERATE STUDENT
HER WINDBREAKER FILTHY CLUTCHING THE TRAIN SEAT
    SO TIGHT WE
SAW HER WRISTPULSE IT WAS
LIKE SEEING HER HEART IN COUNTDOWN

ITS NIGHT. THE ELEPHANT OF POETRY [. . .]

In Karl Parker's long poem titled "Horn o' Plenty, or Notes Toward
a Supreme Cornucopia," the rampant use of the Caps Lock Key has the
effect of making the "notes" seem even more note-like, bringing to mind
Sharpie on Post-Its and phrases scrawled on a white board:

IF IMAGINARY FRIENDS DIDN'T EXIST
I would have to invent them

THAT MOVIE WAS SO BAD
IT MADE MY FRIEND
LAUGH AT GENOCIDE

TO BE AND NOT TO BE
NO QUESTION ABOUT IT

The Caps Lock Key is a more humorous use of typeface than italics,
but wielded carefully, it can convey the same sense of urgent profun-
dity as the latter.

Ten-Dollar Words

While a ten-dollar word (a multisyllabic "vocabulary" word) is not a move in isolation, a stacking up of Ten-Dollar Words is. For example, from "Within This Book, Called Marguerite" by Marjorie Welish: "As time separates us / from the evaporating architectonics to sweeten mythopoetic / substances, you start to count heroically, / hurled down upon a profile of an as yet / unrevealed know-how." This pushes past erudite showboating to a kind of comical Latinate jargon. As with the Throwaway Pun, awareness is key. Ten-Dollar Words, along with alliteration, should never be used humorlessly.

Definition by Negation

Definition by Negation, and its variant Description by Negation, define or describe a thing by way of telling you what the thing is not, rather than what it is; the thing is described by the shape of the hole. For example: From "This Is Not About Pears" by Matthew Hittinger: "whole sections left white, not blank, / but the white where light lifts form / into pears (even though this is not / about pears)" and, from "Lessons in Stalking" by Michele Battiste: "Caveat: This is not a charted series of locations. This is not some coded spygame—pubescent, discarded, outgrown. This is not about getting close or being loved." Whether intentionally or not, Definition by Negation poems seem to reference "Keeping Things Whole" by Mark Strand (first stanza below):

In a field
I am the absence
of field.
This is
always the case.
Wherever I am
I am what is missing.

Definition by Negation belongs to a poetics of surprise—everyone knows what death or the moon is like, but do they know what it *isn't* like?—but after Strand the move is rarely very surprising.

Illogical Causation

Another move that pivots on surprise, Illogical Causation uses the mathematical syntax of causative statements, (e.g., "If x, then y," "Because x, y," "X, so y," and so on), but abandons known logic on the semantic level, as in this line from "Cryptozoology" by Sabrina Orah Mark: "Walter B. was so relieved he slept in his boots." Or, in another example, from Mark Wallace's *Nothing Happened and Besides I Wasn't There*, "I'm so bored with this / that I can't stop." The effect does not follow from the purported cause. Illogical Causation is often seen in playful, "surreal," or cartoon-like poems, especially of the prose variety. However, it needn't be played for laughs or cuteness, but can be used to illustrate patterns of thought (as frequently irrational as not) and perception, in which gaps often exist between events and known causes.

Ending with an End

Ending with an End mimics the recording studio effect that finishes a song by lowering the volume till it "disappears." Poems that End with an End may trail off, fade to black, feature a death (or a closing or exit of some kind), or literally spell out "The End." See Harryette Mullen's "Bleeding Hearts": "Where I live's a wren shack. Pull back. Show wreck. Black fade." Or several examples from my own work: "Desire explodes and the last thing it feels / is every point touching something" ("Camera Obscura"); "then fall uncontrollably back to sleep" ("Must-See Movie"); "Most commonly named wish that is also a fear: / to die in one's sleep" ("I Even Feel Tired in My Dreams"); "How does my X-ray vision / know when to stop? I // was trying to get to the way end" ("Poem with a Superpower"). I am inordinately fond of Ending with an End.

Author's Note: Many of these examples first appeared in a blog post entitled "Moves in Contemporary Poetry," which appeared on HTML Giant. I would like to thank Mike Young for his contributions to the original post as well as HTML Giant for hosting it.

Works Cited

Aquiline, Danielle. "Autobiogeography." *Eleventh Muse* Jan. 2007: 1. Print.

Barrett, Terry. *Criticizing Art: Understanding the Contemporary*. Mountain View: Mayfield, 1994. Print.

Battiste, Michele. "Lessons in Stalking." *Diagram* 2.3. Web.

Boehl, Dan. *Work*. Columbus: Pavement Saw, 2007. Print.

Božičević, Ana. *Stars of the Night Commute*. Grafton, VT: Tarpaulin Sky, 2009. Print.

Brock-Broido, Lucie. *The Master Letters*. New York: Alfred A. Knopf, 1997. Print.

———. *Trouble in Mind*. New York: Alfred A. Knopf, 2004. Print.

Chiasson, Dan. "My Ravine." *Legitimate Dangers: American Poets of the New Century*. Eds. Michael Dumanis and Cate Marvin. Louisville: Sarabande, 2006: 68. Print.

———. "Vermont." *Legitimate Dangers: American Poets of the New Century*. Eds. Michael Dumanis and Cate Marvin. Louisville: Sarabande, 2006: 69. Print.

Christle, Heather. *The Difficult Farm*. Denver: Octopus, 2009. Print.

Cohen, Julia and Mathias Svalina. "Only So Much Fits in a Petri Dish." *Past Simple* 4. Feb. 2008. Web.

Compton, Shanna. *Down Spooky*. Austin: Winnow, 2005. Print.

Ebert, Roger. "Why I Hate 3-D (And You Should Too)." *Newsweek*, 30. April, 2010. Web.

Emmanuel, Lynn. "Dear Final Journey." *Boston Review* 34.4 (2009): 18. Print.

Fjeld, Jessica. *On Animate Life: Its Profligacy, Organ Meats, Etc.* New York: Poetry Society of America, 2006. Print.

Fulton, Alice. *Sensual Math*. New York: Norton, 1995. Print.

Gabbert, Elisa. *The French Exit*. Austin: Birds LLC, 2010. Print.

Harmon, Joshua. *Scape*. Boston: Black Ocean, 2009. Print.

Hittinger, Matthew. *Pear Slip*. New York: Spire, 2007. Print.

Leon, Jon. *Hit Wave*. New York: Kitchen, 2008. Print.

Lerner, Ben. "Mad Lib Elegy." *Poetry Foundation*. Web. 15 Aug. 2010.

Lin, Tao. "an easy way to eat a lot of calories is to eat a block of cheese." *The Lifted Brow* 4. 17 Jan. 2009. Print.

Mark, Sabrina Orah. *Tsim Tsum*. Ardmore, PA: Saturnalia, 2009. Print.

Marks, Justin. *A Million in Prizes*. Kalamazoo: New Issues, 2009. Print.

Mazer, Ben. *Poems*. Boston: Pen & Anvil, 2010. Print.

McDaniel, Jeffrey. "Play It Again, Salmonella." *American Poetry: The Next Generation*. Eds. Gerald Costanzo and Jim Daniels. Pittsburgh: Carnegie Mellon UP, 2000. 264. Print.

Mullen, Harryette. *Sleeping With The Dictionary*. Berkeley: U of California P, 2002. Print.

Nealon, Chris. *Plummet*. Washington, D.C.: Edge, 2009. Print.

Parker, Alan Michael. "The Vandals." *Legitimate Dangers: American Poets of the New Century*. Eds. Michael Dumanis and Cate Marvin. Louisville: Sarabande, 2006. 282. Print.

Parker, Karl. *Personationskin*. Reston, VA: No Tell, 2009. Print.

Perelman, Bob. *Ten to One: Selected Poems*. Middletown, CT: Wesleyan UP, 1999. Print.

Powell, D. A. "[when you touch down upon this earth. little reindeers]." *Legitimate Dangers: American Poets of the New Century*. Eds. Michael Dumanis and Cate Marvin. Louisville: Sarabande, 2006. 286. Print.

Spaar, Lisa Russ. "Whether." *Ploughshares* 35.4 (2009): 163. Print.

Starkweather, Sampson. *The Heart Is Green from So Much Waiting*. Brooklyn: Immaculate Disciples, 2010. Print.

Stafford, William. "Traveling Through the Dark." *Contemporary American Poetry*. Ed. A. Poulin, Jr. Boston: Houghton, 1996. 563. Print.

Stevens, Wallace. *Collected Poetry and Prose*. New York: Library of America, 1997. Print.

Strand, Mark. "Keeping Things Whole." *Contemporary American Poetry*. Ed. A. Poulin, Jr. Boston: Houghton, 1996. 584. Print.

Svalina, Mathias. *Why I Am White*. New York: Kitchen, 2007. Print.

Wallace, Mark. *Nothing Happened and Besides I Wasn't There*. Washington, D.C.: Edge, 1997. Print.

Welish, Marjorie. *The Annotated "Here" and Selected Poems*. Minneapolis: Coffee House, 2000. Print.

Wise, Suzanne. "Confession." *Legitimate Dangers: American Poets of the New Century*. Eds. Michael Dumanis and Cate Marvin. Louisville: Sarabande, 2006. 422. Print.

An Aesthetics of Accumulation:
On the Contemporary Litany

Michael Dumanis

Consider, preferably through reading it out loud, Lisa Jarnot's poem "Song of the Chinchilla," from her collection *Ring of Fire*:

You chinchilla in the marketplace in france
you international chinchilla, chinchilla of the
plains and mountains all in fur you fur of the
chinchilla of the pont de neuf, selling wrist
watches, on the oldest bridge of evolution that
you are, you, chinchilla, going roadside towards
the cars, the dark arabian chinchilla of the
neutral zone with pears, you still life of
chinchilla, abstractions of chinchilla, aperitif
chinchilla, lowing in the headlands in my mind,
dark, the cliffs of dover, dark chinchilla, tractor
of chinchilla, chili of chinchilla, chill of the
chinchilla, crosswalk of chinchilla of the dawn,
facilitator you, chinchilla, foodstuffs for the
food chain dressed in light.

Each time I enter this poem, I am overcome with both a childlike fancy and the kind of mild rapture that I, despite a lack of religious conviction, can't help but feel in the presence of stained glass, Baroque cupolas, and high church windows. Various religious traditions utilize the repetition of words or phrases to enact spiritual transformation, and I feel as though the language has cast on me a spell, or, more precisely, since the poem employs a second person address from the start, I feel as though the language has cast me *into* a spell, that something mystical is taking place—the incantation of a shaman—and I am fully implicated in it. The word "chinchilla" recurs fifteen times in the space of fifteen lines until it no longer references an absurdly-named small furry mammal and transforms into a kind of mantra, a catalyst for the phrases it calls into being, a firm organizing principle that serves to rein in somewhat the disjunctive cacophony around it.

Each successive iteration of the word "chinchilla" intensifies the power of the repeated word over the surrounding language; while one can make literal meaning fairly easily at the poem's outset (the addressee is in a marketplace, is all in fur, is moving toward traffic, etc.), by the tenth line of the poem, the list of chinchilla-related remarks begins to shed its final shreds of sense, succumbing to the chant of the catalytic mantra: "chili of chinchilla, chill of the / chinchilla." Likewise, the manic repetition of "chinchilla" as organizing principle seems to trigger other repetitions in the poem, creating a cat's cradle of sonic patterns and associations: four different lines end identically with "of the"; the word "you" recurs seven times; "arabian" assonantially triggers "abstractions" and "aperitif"; "all in fur" folds into "you fur of the / chinchilla," and "pont de neuf" (the oldest standing bridge over the Seine in Paris) morphs and translates itself into "bridge of evolution."

What if you were to replace the word "chinchilla" with your given name? Picking a name at random: "You alicia in the marketplace in france / you international alicia, alicia of the / plains and mountains all in fur ... you still life of / alicia, abstractions of alicia, aperitif / alicia, lowing in the headlands in my mind ..." If your name is Alicia, until we get to the chinchilla-generated "chili" and "chill," the poem begins to make a peculiar kind of sense. It functions as a travelogue listing both literal and metaphysical locales in which the self is being located or dislocated, a delineation of the boundaries of the self, a conjurer's spell calling the self—whether Alicia or you or something called a chinchilla—into being.

In a way, "Song of the Chinchilla" seems extremely self-generative and dislocating, an engine fueled by the word "chinchilla" that will continue chugging however long the writer chooses to inject more fuel into its lines, a perpetual motion machine that can transport us into any direction the word "chinchilla" triggers. On the other hand, the poem also paradoxically feels remarkably static and focused, yoked to the word "chinchilla," obsessively yoyo-ing back to its starting place, not capable of straying from the object of its concentration. This is the paradox of a poem advanced on the fuel of repetition: on the one hand, this is the most open of forms, a resistance of any kind of closure, a kind of immortality for the poem if the poem so chooses because it can keep perpetuating its motion endlessly, but on the other hand, this is the most self-limiting of forms, a poem that can never fly off all that far from its trigger, essentially, a poem on a leash. Thus the repeated word that drives the poem is both enabling the writer to leap wildly while simultaneously keeping the writer from moving at all.

That tension can be illustrated perhaps even more acutely through another poem by Lisa Jarnot, "The United States of America," from her collection *Black Dog Songs*:

> I'm going to ask you to transition into a new theme about
> the war. The thing that comes to mind now is the war:
> the big war, the little war, the war that's in my head,
> the war around the edges of my ears, the war to kill
> the troops, the war to kill the cows, the transitional war,
> the bloody war, the not-bloody war, the semi-bloody war,
> the figure of the neighborhood with war, running toward
> the herds of cattle in the war, not good at war, awash in war,
> the war-to-mores, the more and more to war.

The war central to America's consciousness and conscience at the time of the poem's publication is conjured into the poem through incantatory, obsessive repetition. The phrase "to transition into a new theme about / the war" locks the poem in its new theme's clutches regardless of how associative, jumpy, and self-generative successive phrases may be, so much so that even the word "transition" cannot be fully gotten past, the poem transitioning back to it after several lines with "the transitional war." War remains the poem's only landscape, whether it's in the head or in the fields, little or big, bloody or only somewhat bloody.

The Jarnot poems "Song of the Chinchilla" and "The United States of America" are two examples of the anaphoric litany, a poetic form which can be traced to the Old Testament (notably to the Song of Songs, Ecclesiastes, and the Book of Psalms) and through both the Christian spiritual tradition and English literary history (in such familiar places as The Sermon on the Mount, the opening lines of Charles Dickens's *A Tale of Two Cities*, the famous and oft-used example of Christopher Smart's eighteenth-century 74-line anaphoric ode to his cat "For I Will Consider My Cat Jeoffry" (a section from the longer poem *Jubilate Agno*), Walt Whitman's *Leaves of Grass*, and Martin Luther King's "I Have a Dream" speech), and which appears with a fairly remarkable degree of frequency in contemporary poetry. Anaphora, an ancient Greek word literally meaning "carrying back," was defined by Cicero as the technique of beginning successive lines with the same word or phrase, but has since expanded to also include the act of beginning successive neighboring clauses with identical language, a form of parallelism which causes the repetition (as opposed to content) to serve as the organizing principle and common starting point for successive units. A litany, originally derived from the Greek words for prayer and entreaty, and initially specifically denoting a liturgical prayer consisting of a series of petitions recited by a leader alternating with responses by the congregation, began by the early nineteenth century to simply mean a long repeated series, as in a litany of wrongs or a litany of curses.

In poetry, a litany, broadly defined, is an incantatory, recitative poem held together through the obsessive repetition of the same words, phrases, or syntactical patterns. While litanies are frequently anaphoric, they need not necessarily be. Stephen Burt's "Paysage Moralisé," from his collection *Parallel Play*, is an epiphoric (!) litany where every line ends with the word "place" or a near-homophone thereof (such as "plays" or "sewn-up lace"):

> Mom and Dad must have believed they had found a safe place:
> The ten- and twelve-year-olds they could place
> In the neighborhood schools, the teens who would take their place

> In a few years, and the young adults who would replace
> Themselves if all went well could each find a place
> In this frivolous landscape, which nonetheless offered no place
> Without its form of scrutiny. Sneakers displaced [. . .]

In Burt's litany, the inevitable journey of each line toward its source-word, the yoking back, is especially evident as every line can only head one way, obsessively returning, as in a sestina or ghazal, to the particular endword's inevitable closure. Alternately, "sweet reader, flanneled and tulled," the opening poem of Olena Kalytiak Davis's second book, *shattered sonnets love cards and other off and back handed importunities,* presented in lieu of a dedication page for the whole book, uses the word "reader" as its trigger word as many times as it can get away with, interrupting lines to reiterate its address, obsessively entreating the reader by naming him at unexpected points. The poem begins,

> Reader unmov'd and Reader unshaken, Reader unseduc'd
> and unterrified, through the long-loud and the sweet-still
> I creep toward you. Toward you, I thistle and I climb.

> I crawl, Reader, servile and cervine, through this blank
> season, counting—I sleep and I sleep. I sleep,
> Reader, toward you, loud as a cloud and deaf, Reader, deaf

> as a leaf [. . .]

The continuous, obsessive repetition of the word "Reader" (which occurs thirty-nine times over the course of the poem's fifty-four lines, with as many as six instances of the word in a single tercet) functions as a kind of incantatory seduction spell, lulling (if successful) the unsuspecting reader into the poem's clutches. It is as though, with every iteration, the poem calls the reader into being through a continual intimate entreaty, establishing him as someone as-yet-unseduced-and-unaffected whom the poem, through the thistle-and-climb of its language will attempt to woo. Davis is creating a self-generating sonic landscape here: the words in her litany generate other words, creating the poem out of itself: "leaf" and "deaf" exist in the above lines because of "loud" and "cloud" and make a kind of sound-sense rather than a literal sense. Davis has given language full dominion here, has made sound the organizing principle that gives a structure to the otherwise disordered.

While litanies no longer signify liturgical call-and-response, they nonetheless at times retain the litany's etymological root in prayer and entreaty, and the litany's tone is often not only obsessive but also devotional and/or ecstatic. The litany's language is forever shamanistically calling something into being, giving it shape through incantation. In Mark Jarman's anaphoric "Unholy Sonnet #17" in *Unholy Sonnets,* a poem about the erotic nature of complete religious devotion (or, conversely, about the spirituality inherent in sexual congress), that-which-is-summoned-through-language is literally God:

> God like a kiss, God like a welcoming,
> God like a hand guiding another hand
> And raising it or making it descend,
> God like the pulse point and its silent drumming,
> And the tongue going to it, God like the humming
> Of pleasure if the skin felt it as sound,
> God like the hidden wanting to be found
> And like the joy of being and becoming.
> And God the understood, the understanding,
> And God the pressure trying to relieve
> What is not pain but names itself with weeping,
> And God the rush of time and God time standing,
> And God the touch body and soul believe,
> And God the secret neither one is keeping.

The repeated "God" always takes the greatest stress of any line that includes it, a punctuation to the poem's rhythm which serves as more of a unifying mechanism than the sonnet form and rhyme scheme. "God" is what we keep returning to and redefining and intensifying, through our revisitations, our understanding of. Jarman enacts through the anaphora that "humming / Of pleasure if the skin felt it as sound," where by the end of the poem, the pileup of the "And God" anaphora begins to sound like an interjection of sexual pleasure. Subtly, Jarman introduces a *volta,* or turn, after eight lines, through varying the anaphora from "God like" to "And God," right after the word "becoming"— for the remaining six lines, metaphor replaces simile and the poem becomes louder, more ecstatic, and God becomes understood, becomes "the touch body and soul believe."

A more freewheeling and at-first-glance secular but similarly ecstatic and obsessive litany is French Surrealist Andre Breton's conjuring-through-language of his wife, "Free Union," here excerpted from a David Antin translation in Michael Benedikt's *The Poetry of Surrealism: An Anthology*, which begins:

My wife whose hair is a brush fire
Whose thoughts are summer lightning
Whose waist is an hourglass
Whose waist is the waist of an otter caught in the teeth of a tiger
Whose mouth is a bright cockade with the fragrance of a star of the
    first magnitude
Whose teeth leave prints like the tracks of white mice over snow
Whose tongue is made out of amber and polished glass
Whose tongue is a stabbed wafer
The tongue of a doll with eyes that open and shut
Whose tongue is an incredible stone
My wife whose eyelashes are strokes in the handwriting of a child
Whose eyebrows are nests of swallows [. . .]

I say at-first-glance-secular because the language here directly calls to mind one of the anaphoric sections from The Song of Songs:

Behold, thou art fair, my love; behold, thou art fair; thou hast doves'
    eyes within thy locks: thy hair is as a flock of goats, that appear
    from Mount Gilead.
Thy teeth are like a flock of sheep that are even shorn, which came up
    from the washing; whereof every one bear twins, and none is
    barren among them.
Thy lips are like a thread of scarlet, and thy speech is comely: thy
    temples are like a piece of a pomegranate within thy locks.
Thy neck is like the tower of David built for an armory, whereon
    there hang a thousand bucklers, all shields of mighty men.
Thy two breasts are like two young roes that are twins, which feed
    among the lilies. [. . .] (4.1–5)

In both selections, the beloved is being created through the cataloging of a surreal menagerie, the language generating the beloved out of an inexhaustible anaphoric catalog of wonders. The ability of the speaker to go on for however long he wishes in cataloging the beloved's extraordinary features makes the beloved, like God, into all things. The Breton poem ends, "My wife with eyes that are the equal of water and air and earth and fire." The litany operates inductively: by rattling off all of the metaphors for the wife's features with increasing hyperbole, Breton has made her an amalgam of all the elements and is able to make the wife's eyes equivalent to all matter. A third excellent example of the litany as generative catalog is Kenneth Koch's exuberant litany "Alive for an Instant," which similarly defines the self through increasingly hyperbolic metaphor, beginning by fragmenting the self into a world of animals—"I have a bird in my head and a pig in my stomach / And a flower in my genitals and a tiger in my genitals / And a lion in my genitals and I am after you but I have a song in my heart / And my song is a dove"— and ends self-referentially as an ars poetica of sorts, defining the self as all poets, referencing the litany as a maelstrom, and asking how all of the animals made it into the poem, then positing that this type of writing accomplishes three things: resurrection, insurrection, and inspiration:

> I am Lord Byron I am Percy Shelley I am Ariosto
> I eat the bacon I went down the slide I have a thunderstorm in my
>   inside I will never hate you
> But how can this maelstrom be appealing? do you like menageries?
>   my god
> Most people want a man! So here I am
> I have a pheasant in my reminders I have a goshawk in my clouds
> Whatever is it which has led all these animals to you?
> A resurrection? or maybe an insurrection? an inspiration?
> I have a baby in my landscape and I have a wild rat in my secrets from
>   you.

In litanies, the simultaneous coexistence of a variety of statements that can be made about a specific thing (be it a chinchilla, a war, Christopher Smart's cat, or Andre Breton's wife) takes the place of any kind of narrative cause-and-effect. It is often possible to move around the order of the repetitions of a litany poem's midsection without disrupting the poem's flow or obfuscating the poem's meaning. And yet, despite the lack of narrative causation, the litany feels anything but static, gathering kinetic energy through the maximalist, expansive piling-on of modifiers to the repeated words—a snowball gathering size and speed as it avalanches down a hill. The following excerpts from Allen Ginsberg's litany "America" serve as an excellent example both of the democratic, non-hierarchic relationship of the poem's individual lines to one another and of the kinetic, energy-accumulating, maximalist quality of most litanies:

America when will we end the human war?
Go fuck yourself with your atom bomb.
I don't feel good don't bother me.
I won't write my poem till I'm in my right mind.
America when will you be angelic?
When will you take off your clothes?
When will you look at yourself through the grave?
When will you be worthy of your million Trotskyites?

[. . .]

America you don't really want to go to war.
America it's them bad Russians.
Them Russians them Russians and them Chinamen. And them Russians.
The Russia wants to eat us alive. The Russia's power mad. She wants to take our cars from out our garages.
Her wants to grab Chicago. Her needs a Red Reader's Digest. Her wants our auto plants in Siberia. Him big bureaucracy running our fillingstations.
That no good. Ugh. Him makes Indians learn read. Him need big black niggers. Hah. Her make us all work sixteen hours a day. Help.
America this is quite serious. [. . .]

The organizing principle here makes the poem less a cause-and-effect sequence and more a Cornell box of declarative statements. As with Jarnot's address to the chinchilla, the address to America becomes progressively more intimate with each naming. Here, however, it is the surrounding language that gradually acquires more power over the word "America"—perhaps because of the truly anaphoric positioning of "America" at the outset of lines (as opposed to Jarnot's interweaving of "war" and "chinchilla" into the middles of heavily enjambed lines) which causes each line to end-stop far away from the originating word before being abruptly yoked back to it, "America" succumbing under the weight of what the speaker has to say in his address, its anaphora occasionally giving way to other anaphoras (such as the repetitions of "When will you" in the first excerpt and the repetitions of "Them Russians," "The

Russia," "Him," and "Her" in the comic grammatical collapse of the second excerpt). The statements are discreet from one another, statements radically varying in tone and length made parallel and ordered through the anaphoric organizing principle. Ginsberg is acquiring energy here not just from the repetition, but from the variation.

One could argue, especially after repeated readings of "America," that there is something ontologically pluralistic and democratic about the litany as a form. It's the rhetorical structure of the Declaration of Independence, the rhetorical structure of most of the U.S. Constitution. There is no hierarchical relationship between one anaphoric iteration and another, merely the binding glue of similar sounds. Language is what binds together what is otherwise potentially extremely fragmentary and disjointed. Language is the organizing principle, rather than story or self. Parallel patterns of repetitive syntax and diction can order the disorderly with remarkable ease and allow for an extremely high degree of disjunction. Jennifer L. Knox's comically absurdist "The Opposite of Crunchberries" from her collection *A Gringo Like Me* holds together completely disparate objects through a repetitive "The opposite of ___ is ___" construction:

> The opposite of Crunchberries is
>   fried chicken.
> The opposite of fried chicken is
>   geometry class.
> The opposite of geometry class is
>   an otter.
> The opposite of an otter is
>   William Shatner [. . .]

Another, perhaps more unusual, example of the litany's singular use of language as binding glue for the otherwise-fragmented is Dean Young's cento "If Thou Dislik'st What Thou First Light'st Upon," the first poem in his 1999 *First Course in Turbulence*, a litany composed for the most part from the transcription, in alphabetical order, of the index to poems beginning with the letter "I" in the *Norton Anthology of Poetry*:

> I had come to the house, in a cave of trees,
> I had dreamed of the perfect gray pants,

I have a life that did not become,
a young sister made of glass.
I have done it again.
I like a church, I like a cowl,
I like the look of agony.
I love the old melodious lays,
I love it when they demonstrate the oxygen masks,
never messing up their hair.
I met the Bishop on the road,
In a coign of the cliff between high and low,
In a dark time,
Among wolves and periwinkles,
In a station of the metro,
In Breughel's great painting, *The Kermess.*
Indeed I must confess,
Indigo, magenta, color of ghee,
what the hell is the color of ghee? [. . .]

Out of the I-triggered opening fragments of other poets, Young inductively constructs an all-encompassing, whole self. Whereas the self of Koch's litany consisted of a menagerie of animals, here the organizing mechanism that amalgamates a self from the building blocks of other poems, uniting them into one opening poem through the anaphoric repetition of the letter I.

A litany, as a form, feels remarkably postmodern in its non-hierarchic and non-linear relationship of individual lines, its fragmentation and reconstitution of identity without relying on a coherent first person speaker, its inherent ability to keep going and resist closure through extending the anaphora, its impulse to list and catalog and generate rather than narrate or otherwise causally link. These qualities may help explain the form's seeming popularity with numerous contemporary poets. All of these qualities are on exhibit, for example, in the four-page title poem of Endi Bogue Hartigan's debut collection *One Sun Storm*, winner of the Colorado Prize for Poetry. The eponymous litany begins each of its lines with the anaphora "One" (as though we're taking an inventory, or as though we're trying to count but find ourselves incapable of ever reaching the number two), interrupting the anaphora only with the likewise-anaphoric interruptions "Impossible break" and "Impossible speak," and with quotes about sunstorms from the websites of NASA and the National Center for Atmospheric Research. Hartigan begins her catalog,

> One stormland
> One arc and one plume rising from the sea of your storms
> One hand holding one head, one vessel drifting
> Impossible break
> One public meeting, the doldrums of voices in the quorum
> One algae-filled fish tank through which one streetlight gleams
> One mark of pain that marks the deepest wood
> One stormland
> "These diagrams... don't rely on any assumptions about what the
>   spectrum looks like."
> One person torn from one person's interior [. . .]

The poem draws attention to the litany's role as an enumerator, accruing energy and meaning through the accumulation of disparate iterations brought into alignment through their anaphora. The lines do not have an inherently causal or hierarchic relationship with one another, and the poem is content to keep gaining momentum through its list, never reaching after closure, ending its incantatory catalog as abruptly as it began: "One stormland, one arc, one plume / One fish line thrown wrongly and loosening / The pulse of one hand, and one hand / One flake of green paint off the wood / One sun described every day to one end, one immersion / One voice rising and falling in one chorus / One forest of light through one fern."

A recent collection that very effectively uses the litany form throughout to create a kind of non-hierarchical inventory of experience, a unifying organizing principle through which to process the dissociative white noise of the world, is Juliana Spahr's *This Connection of Everyone with Lungs*, a book consisting of two litanies, the eight-page "Poem Written After September 11, 2001" and the near-booklength "Poem Written from November 30, 2002 to March 27, 2003," which lists, in a diary format repeatedly addressed to the speaker's "Beloveds," the particulars of the events of a particular day in a world-at-war that the speaker is observing without engaging in. The entry "March 5, 2003" begins,

> When I wake up this morning the world is a series of isolated,
>   burning fires as it is every morning.

It burns in Israel where ten died from a bomb on a bus.

Yesterday it also burned in the Philippines where twenty-one died from a bomb at an airport. And then it burned some more a few hours later outside a health clinic in a nearby city, killing one.

It burns and the Pope urges everyone to fast and pray for peace because it is Ash Wednesday.

It burns in Cambodia, which has closed its border with Thailand.

It burns in a fistfight between delegates at the Islamic emergency summit.

It burns in the West Bank and the Gaza Strip.

It burns in the form of Israeli-imposed closures that cause severe economic problems for Palestinians.

It burns in North Korea.

This is the stuff of the everyday in this world.

In this never ending twentieth century world. [. . .]

Spahr uses anaphoric construction to connect all of the world's fires, to argue that all tragedies are linked because all people are linked (as the language itself is linked), to argue that the geographic location and particulars of the way a particular fire rages are less significant than the fact of the fire itself. In her "January 28, 2003," Spahr uses the repetition of the word exist to merely list that which does exist, according to her radio, without further comment:

Today, on the radio, Christie Brinkley exists and her worries about Billy Joel's driving abilities exist.

A lawsuit exists where Catherine Zeta Jones and Michael Douglas are suing *Hello!* Magazine for poor quality wedding photos.

U2 spy planes exist flying over the Koreas.

Supermodel Gisele Bundchen's plan to eradicate hunger in Brazil exists.

[. . .]

Bronze Age highways in Iraq, Syria and Turkey continue to exist.

Renée Zellweger and Richard Gere, lead actors in Chicago, exist.

Cell phones and tunnel vision exists.

Cable problems exist in a crash in Charlotte.

A dismembered mother, the shoe bomber's letters, Scott Peterson's wife and girlfriend, Brian Patrick Regan's letters to Hussein and Gadhafi, nineteen thousand gallons of crude oil in the frozen Nemadji River, all of this exists.

The world goes on and on, spins tighter and then looser on a wobbling axis, and it has a list of adjectives to describe it, such as various and beautiful and new, but neither light, nor certitude, nor peace exist.

While Juliana Spahr's poems turn into catalogs of atrocities, even in those moments they seek to underscore, through anaphoric parallelism, the interconnectedness of all events and experiences. "Poem Written After September 11, 2001" begins by cataloging that which exists universally: "There are these things: // cells, the movement of cells and the division of cells // and then the general beating of circulation // and hands, and body, and feet // [. . .] // There is a space around the hands and space in the room. // There is space in the room that surrounds the shapes of everyone's hands and body and feet and cells and the beating contained within." The poem proceeds to use the anaphora "as everyone with lungs breathes" to enact the shared use of the space between us, repeating what has just been said and extending it, unspooling the reader's breath, out from the starting-place, further. Language is used to link all people the way Spahr posits that breath links all people:

Everyone with lungs breathes the space in and out as everyone with lungs breathes the space between the hands in and out
as everyone with lungs breathes the space between the hands and the space around the hands in and out

as everyone with lungs breathes the space between the hands and the space around the hands in and the space of the room in and out

as everyone with lungs breathes the space between the hands and the space around the hands in and the space of the room and the space of the building that surrounds the room in and out

[. . .]

as everyone with lungs breathes the space between the hands and the space around the hands in and the space of the room and the

> space of the building that surrounds the room and the space of
> the neighborhoods nearby and the space of the cities and the
> space of the regions and the space of the nations and the space of
> the continents and islands and the space of the oceans and the
> space of the troposphere and the space of the stratosphere and
> the space of the mesosphere in and out.

Spahr's use of repetition simultaneously as incantation, as a way to connect the disconnected with the binding power of language, and as a way of creating a non-hierarchic inventory of experience underscores how much potential exists in the litany form. I would like to close by considering a litany that seems to be lurking in the shadows of Spahr's book, the booklength poem *Alphabet* by the late Danish poet Inger Christensen. Like Spahr, Christensen uses the litany form to unspool an inventory of that which exists. However, Christensen adds two additional organizing principles—alphabetical progression and the Fibonacci sequence. The poem is in fourteen sections, the line-length of each section—as in Fibonacci—equaling the sum of the previous two section's line-lengths, each section introducing another letter and the words it creates, from a to n. Christensen conjures the world into being, her first section serving as a simple, arguably joyous declaration of praise for the wonders of creation: "apricot trees exist, apricot trees exist," she writes. The second section brings in the letter b, and mixes the chemical world with the apricot trees: "bracken exists; and blackberries, blackberries; bromine exists; and hydrogen, hydrogen." The madcap listing of that-which-is, increasingly sounding more desperate as the lists, due to Fibonacci, get longer and longer, stresses the fragility and conditionality of each object's existence. The catalog of the natural world becomes increasingly more menacing to the apricot trees: "doves exist, dreamers, and dolls; killers exist, and doves, and doves; haze, dioxin, and days; days exist, days and death; and poems exist; poems, days, death," and, by section eleven, "hydrogen bombs exist / a plea to die."

Works Cited
Breton, Andre. Trans. David Antin. "Free Union." *The Poetry of Surrealism: An Anthology*. Ed. Michael Benedikt. Boston, MA: Little Brown, 1974. Print.

Burt, Stephen. *Parallel Play*. Minneapolis, MN: Graywolf, 2006. Print.

Christensen, Inger. *Alphabet*. Trans. Susanna Nied. New York: New Directions, 2001. Print.

Davis, Olena Kalytiak. *Shattered Sonnets, Love Cards, And Other Off-And-Back Handed Importunities*. Portland, OR: Tin House, 2003. Print.

Ginsberg, Allen. *Howl and Other Poems*. San Francisco, CA: City Lights Editions, 1956. Print.

Hartigan, Endi Bogue. *One Sun Storm*. Fort Collins, CO: Center for Literary Publishing, 2010. Print.

The Holy Bible. Cambridge: Cambridge UP, 1995. Print. Authorized King James Vers.

Jarman, Mark. *Unholy Sonnets*. Ashland, OR: Story Line, 2003. Print.

Jarnot, Lisa. *Black Dog Songs*. Chicago, IL: Flood Editions, 2003. Print.

Jarnot, Lisa. *Ring of Fire*. Cambridge, MA: Zoland, 2001. Print.

Knox, Jennifer. *A Gringo Like Me*. New York: Soft Skull, 2005. Print.

Koch, Kenneth. *On the Great Atlantic Railway: Collected Poems, 1950-1988*. New York: Knopf, 1996. Print.

Spahr, Juliana. *This Connection of Everyone with Lungs*. Berkeley, CA: U of California P, 2005. Print.

Young, Dean. *First Course in Turbulence*. Pittsburgh, PA: U of Pittsburgh P, 1999. Print.

Cornucopia, or, Contemporary American Rhyme

Stephen Burt

A s a proportion of all published verse, fewer American poems use rhyme, and even fewer use forms that require end-rhymes, than was the case thirty—never mind, eighty—years ago. I want to show not exactly why that happened, but what that change means for how we hear rhyme and for how it gets used, in the United States, by the most interesting poets who use it now. (My argument does not apply to the contemporary poets of Britain and Ireland, though the terms I define might help you think about their poems too.) I hope you'll forgive me for starting long ago and far away: I'll get contemporary, and American, as soon as I can.

Rhyme used to be the norm: it came into English *as* a norm, along with a lot of French words, in the cross-channel exchanges that also created Middle English. Since rhyme was a "modern," Continental, vernacular device, Renaissance classicizers wrote against it, either seriously or satirically, as in Ben Jonson's "A Fit of Rhyme Against Rhyme":

> Greek was free from rhyme's infection,
> Happy Greek by this protection
> > Was not spoiled.
> Whilst the Latin, queen of tongues,
> Is not yet free from rhyme's wrongs,
> > But rests foiled.

The joke would be no joke unless we expected that poems in English, in general, in Jonson's day, would rhyme: we lose track of the fact that it rhymes, until the poem reminds us, over and over, by telling us that it should not. The effect is like hearing somebody giving a speech in favor of nudism, but refusing to take off his clothes: rhyme that would otherwise stay near the background moves, once we understand the sense, to the front.

John Milton defended the absence of rhyme from *Paradise Lost*—that is, he thought its absence required defense: "The measure is English heroic verse without rhyme," he wrote,

> as that of Homer in Greek and of Virgil in Latin; rhyme being no nec-
> essary adjunct or true ornament of poem or good verse, in longer works
> especially, but the invention of a barbarous age. . . . This neglect then of
> rhyme so little is to be taken for a defect, though it may seem so perhaps
> to vulgar readers, that it rather is to be esteemed an example set, the first
> in English, of ancient liberty recovered to heroic poem from the trouble-
> some and modern bondage of rhyming.

"Ancient liberty" meant Greece and Rome, but also England before the Norman conquest, when Francophone invaders supposedly brought absolute monarchy, along with end-rhyme, to the island. Neither import, by Milton's day, looked much like its Continental form: English has many more word endings, hence fewer instances for a given rhyme.

Yet English did find structures, standardized forms, that competent poets could replicate without strain: couplets and quatrains, separately or in combination, became so common that they could pass almost without notice as poets emphasized effects other than rhyme. Here is the first quatrain from Shakespeare's sonnet I:

> From fairest creatures we desire increase
> That thereby beauty's rose might never die,
> But as the riper should by time decease,
> His tender heir might bear his memory.

Rhyme highlights the rhymed words, if only because all verse lines highlight their end words. If you ask why Shakespeare used these rhymes, you can find answers ("increase" anticipates, and counters, "decease"; disyllables balance the monosyllabic "die"). But that might not be the first question you're likely to ask—and if you memorize, or recite, the passage, or compare it with other sonnets from Shakespeare's day, the fact that it rhymes is not going to loom large: rather, quatrain rhyme helps establish the norm against which other verbal effects stand out.

Call it background rhyme. From Chaucer to Shakespeare to the eighteenth century, and for many poets until our own time, rhyme was an element in the "metrical contract," the agreement that poets would deliver a language more tightly organized (and therefore more memorable) than conversation and discursive prose, but the individual rhymes, as rhymes, would not usually draw more attention than other aspects of the verse. Pope's *Essay on Criticism* praised mimetic effects drawn from rhythm and from consonance—"the sound must seem an echo to the sense," as when speedy lines depicted a speedy goddess. But when he discussed rhymes, he praised no special effects they could generate. Instead, he attacked clichés: "If crystal streams 'with pleasing murmurs creep,' / The reader's threatened (not in vain) with 'sleep.' " Those rhymes stood out because they were overfamiliar: rhyme, Pope's *Essay* implies, usually should not stand out at all.

Rhyme is background, unmarked, a feature required by "contract," in plenty of nineteenth-century poetry: inexperienced readers (students, for example) may not notice that Robert Browning's "My Last Duchess" uses rhyming couplets, because the rhymes (hands-stands, said-read) subordinate themselves to every other feature of the poem. W. B. Yeats's "Adam's Curse" (1902) is, among many other things, a passionate defense of background rhyme: "I said, 'A line will take us hours maybe; / Yet if it does not seem a moment's thought / Our stitching and unstitching has been naught.' " Such poetry is not supposed to look like "work," as Yeats says, and the less it looks like work the most successful the work has been. "Rhymes properly used"—so Robert Graves wrote in 1922—"are the good servants whose presence at the dinner-table gives the guests a sense of opulent security; never awkward or over-clever, they handle the dishes silently and professionally. You can trust them not to interrupt the conversation" (6–7). Graves thus defined (though he would not have put it that way) background rhyme, a set of effects that "must on no account appear to guide the sense" nor control the flow of the poem (7).

You can find background rhyme of this kind right up through the twentieth century (students don't notice that W. H. Auden's "Musée de Beaux Arts" rhymes); you can find it frequently in Seamus Heaney, and in other British and Irish poetry, even today. Auden himself later advanced a compact theory of rhyme, writing apropos of Lord Byron's *Don Juan*:

> Words which rhyme, that is to say, words which denote different things but are partially similar in sound, are not necessarily comic. To be comic, the two things they denote must either be so incongruous with each other that one cannot imagine a real situation in which the speaker would need to bring them together, or so irrelevant to each other, that they could only become associated by pure chance. The effect of a comic rhyme is as if the words, on the basis of their auditory friendship, had taken charge of the situation, as if, instead of an event requiring words to describe it, words had the power to create an event. (380)

Auden's description covers much more than just comic (funny) rhyme: it covers all poems in which words, not events, are in charge, and all rhymes that do not seem to have arisen (as if naturally) from the other aspects of the poem. It is close to a definition of what I am going to call foreground rhyme, as well as a claim about how such rhyme works. Near the end of the first canto of *Don Juan*, Byron, or his narrator, at last tells us what sort of poem he's writing:

> My poem's epic, and is meant to be
>   Divided in twelve books; each book containing,
> With love, and war, a heavy gale at sea,
>   A list of ships, and captains, and kings reigning,
> New characters; the episodes are three:
>   A panoramic view of Hell's in training,
> After the style of Virgil and of Homer,
> So that my name of Epic's no misnomer. (I: 200)

Byron is explaining his "epic" verse form, just as Milton explained his, but Byron is kidding. Though he will indeed show battles and ship-wrecks, by this point in *Don Juan* we know that his goals lie very far from the tragic burden of Virgil: his playful, in part satirical, intention comes out in the foregrounded rhymes, which stick out because they are poly-syllabic, because they employ proper nouns (Homer), and because the words they use are sometimes the oddest in their respective lines. (Be-sea-three is a background rhyme, against which containing-reigning-training stands out.) We hear in the foreground rhymes of *Don Juan* a man who is having fun, who cares for the sounds of the language he is assembling, for the stanza as an assemblage of sounds, far more than he can care (or make us care) for the "captains, and kings," the loves, and the wars, he presents.

You can trace both foreground, and background, rhyme through poets who use rhyme, up to our own time. You can find foreground rhyme among modernists, where it can suggest artificial, or counterin-tuitive, structures rather than comic ones: take Marianne Moore's "The Fish" ("The Fish / wade / through black jade"). You can also find long, famous poems with asymmetrical or irregular structures ("The Love Song of J. Alfred Prufrock," for example) that incorporate both fore-ground and background rhyme; and, as with most binary categories in the arts, you can find many cases that could go either way. You can also find some well-handled background rhyme right up to the end of the twentieth century, especially if you look for it among poets with long careers. Richard Wilbur wrote in 2000 that a stand of trees

> Now, in this leafless time, are ships no more,
> Though it would not be hard to take them for
>
> A roadstead full of naked mast and spar
> In which we see now where the crow's nests are. (*Collected Poems* 43)

The rhymes yield meanings if you look for them: "are" becomes a denuded version of "spar": trees in winter like ships' masts without sails, like elderly men, reduced to their last, bare being. But you have to look hard: what stands out are the images and the rhythms, which remain unbroken (by contrast to the bodies they describe). The poem simply sounds as if it were supposed to rhyme because poems in general, or poems by Richard Wilbur, rhyme. "Are" and "spar," "for" and "more," have surely occurred together, and will occur together again, whether or not Wilbur brings them together this way, nor has he distorted anything else about his line (diction, rhythm, syntax, and so on) in order to make the words fit.

Graves described all rhyme as if it were background rhyme; Wilbur, writing in 1950, described his own verse as if all his rhymes were foreground rhymes, saying that they "serve to limit the work of art, and to declare its artificiality: they say 'This is not the world, but a pattern imposed on the world or found in it: this is a partial and provisional attempt'" (Ciardi 7). Such declarations failed to guide most of Wilbur's interpreters, who have often claimed (and they are wrong) that for him, whatever is, is right. James Longenbach instead calls Wilbur "that rare thing: a seriously misunderstood poet," and Wilbur's rhymes, in younger ears than his, have contributed to the misunderstanding (66).

Poets of Wilbur's generation also used foreground rhyme, for comic and for serious effects. In James Merrill's "Self-Portrait with Tyvek Windbreaker" (1995), the poet walks down a Manhattan street wearing that windbreaker, whose back is a map of the world:

> "Great jacket!" strangers on streetcorners impart.
> The Albanian doorman pats it: "Where you buy?"
> Over his ear-splitting drill a hunky guy
> Yells, "Hey, you'll always know where you are, right?"
> "Ever the fashionable cosmopolite,"
> Beams Ray. And "Voilà mon pays"—the carrot-haired
> Girl in the bakery, touching with her finger
> The little orange France above my heart.
>
> Everyman, c'est moi, the whole world's pal!
> The pity is how soon such feelings sour.
> As I leave the gym a smiling-as-if-I-should-know-her
> Teenager—oh but I *mean*, she's wearing "our"
> Windbreaker, and assumes . . . Yet I return her wave
> Like an accomplice. For while all humans aren't
> Countable as equals, we must behave
> As if they were or the spirit dies (Pascal).

These rhymes, like Byron's, are polyglot, polysyllabic, drawn from quoted speech, or from proper nouns: the terms would never have come together absent the poem. The words' similarities are fleeting, arbitrary, like the inconsequential similarities among the many New Yorkers who wear the "same" windbreaker, with its picture of the "same" world. It is a poem whose own predictions for the planet's future approach despair, predictions not quite hidden—in fact, supported—by the jaunty, pianistic artifice.

I suggest here that foreground rhyme has become, for *most* American poets now, the only kind that we can use: its possibilities have expanded immensely, while background rhyme has become, though not unheard of, scarce, and extremely hard to use well. The most inventive Americans who use rhyme these days almost always use foreground rhyme: their rhymes pop out, like Merrill's and like Byron's, however far they stand in other respects from Merrill's (or Byron's) goals (and I will focus here on poets whose work seems to place them far from Merrill indeed). Rhyme in their verse seems consciously artificial—ornamental, or antiquary, or ironic (even sarcastic), or willed, or faux-naif; it almost has to emphasize (as rhyme in prior generations need not have emphasized) the poem as a thing made, and a thing made of language, separable from the world to which it reacts. As a technical resource (as "scheme," in Stephen Cushman's and John Hollander's sense) foreground rhyme can afford to be irregular, occasional rather than structural, continuous with other kinds of consonance and euphony; as a symbol (as "trope") it can signify, not only artifice, but distance from the past, either from prior eras in history, or from the personal past, from childhood, from a time when rhyme was a norm, and did not necessarily make a poem stand out.

I will start with rhyme at its most consciously artificial, even brittle, in Karen Volkman's dense, sometimes baffling sonnets, whose collective title, *Nomina*, points to the philosophical nominalism that underpins her attitudes. The human world, for her, makes only the sense we impose, so that we may as well—however effortfully—make it more beautiful by imposing rhyme:

> Nice knuckle, uncle. Nice hat, hornet.
> Nice is nervouser than eye or at,
> the gone get going, the icons eat
> a lawful loin, an iridescent sweet
>
> glows its grid-iris, the noun forget. (29)

To be a poet is not, for Volkman, to hide one's art: it is to worry at, worry about, that art, and then to wonder whether that art, or any art, is too "nice," too exacting, too divorced from the disarray of the world. Rhyme marks the poem as *unlike* normal speech, and you cannot read it without taking note of that mark: so in Volkman, and so in the irregular and yet structurally necessary ("load-bearing," as architects say) rhymes of Kay Ryan, whose poems almost all use rhyme in the same way. Here is "Atlas," chosen literally by opening her *Selected Poems* at random:

> Extreme exertion
> isolates a person
> from help,
> discovered Atlas.
> Once a certain
> shoulder-to-burden
> ratio collapses,
> there is so little
> others can do:
> they can't
> lend a hand
> with Brazil
> and not stand
> on Peru. (220)

Ryan may sound colloquial, offhand, but nobody (pace Yeats) is going to mistake this construction for a moment's thought. Almost every line rhymes—exertion-person-certain-burden, Atlas-collapses, can't-stand-hand, do-Peru—and we notice the rhymes the more because so few non-rhyming syllables intervene. The poem is technically a sonnet (fourteen lines, and a break in the scheme at line nine), though it doesn't feel like a sonnet, doesn't feel like anything except another example of Ryan's intricate, witty, thin poems, whose primary subject (like Volkman's!) is often the difficulty we have in wringing, from the flux of the world, some sense.

Ryan's rhymes are structural—their recurrence gives aural shape to the whole poem—but they are also irregular, often internal, rather than showing up only at matching line-ends. When most rhyme in new poetry is foreground rhyme—when we no longer see, nor expect to see, rhyme as the norm in which other effects become special—we hear less difference between rhyme as regular recurrence at line ends and rhyme as irregular, occasional, or intralinear. We also hear less distinction between kinds of rhyme schemes that *can* sound natural in English (quatrains, say) and kinds of rhyme schemes that cannot, e.g. extended monorhyme:

> Drive me to the edge in your Mambo Cadillac.
> > turn left at the graveyard and gas that baby, the black
> night ringing with its holy roller scream. I'll clock
> > you on the highway at three a.m., brother, amen, smack
> the road as hard as we can, because I'm gonna crack
> > the world in two . . . (20)

Stunt driving and stunt rhyming, in these lines from "Mambo Cadillac" by Barbara Hamby, seem to be of a piece; both are (supposedly) admirable for their daring, their flip virtuosity, whose stunt-like designs (pace Wilbur) are obviously not found, but made.

Words and events, the order in well-arranged language and the order that belongs to events in the world, do not correspond, not for Ryan, nor for Volkman, nor for Hamby, and it is prideful folly to claim they do: folly, or else naïvete, the thoughts of a child. The *Princeton Encyclopedia of Poetry and Poetics* notes in its entry for rhyme that children produce rhymes "not only spontaneously and happily, but more easily" than they produce other sorts of effects (e.g. alliteration). "At the end of the twentieth century," quips Angela Sorby, "it was still possible to make money writing in rhyme and meter, as long as you aimed at children" (188–89). As rhyme has become unusual in poems for adults, it remains a norm in poems for children, in the poems we might have heard as children (Dr. Seuss, or Mother Goose). That survival in turn affects what poets who write as adults, for adults, do. Consider the faux-naif, uneasily sheltering environment in Lisa Jarnot's "pastoral" quatrains, for example "Harpersfield Song":

> To the sparrows high on tree tops
> fly on sparrows through the hedge stops
> bristle up and fly away
> black crest heads point this way gay
>
> What to do for you is write you
> into this a word for word zoo
> I and you inside the thread
> of the vowels sad and red. (52–53)

Jarnot's titles invoke William Blake, but her sounds derive from Robert Creeley, a pioneer of faux-naif foreground rhyme: "We dream of heaven as a climbing stair," Creeley wrote; "We look at stars and wonder why and where" (560). Nor are Jarnot's programmatic pastorals the only use of rhyme as a trope for childhood: consider Liz Waldner's "Now We Are Sick(x)." Here is the first half:

> My hand is the tree
> beneath the moon
>
> in one hand a fork
> in the other a spoon
>
> My shoes are neat
> beside my bed
>
> ready to eat
> whenever I'm fed (44)

Naïve rhyme here approximates nursery rhyme, as in A. A. Milne's *Now We Are Six,* but to sinister implication: the child seems ready to be unde-ceived, brought to adulthood. Waldner's poem continues:

> Sever this tree
> from the root
>
> bind my hand
> hobble foot—
>
> The moon will note the menu:
> The girl was served
>
> a male hors d'oeuvre
> at a bedside venue (44)

Waldner's lines appear in couplets but rhyme in quatrains (abab cdcd efef ghhg). The rhymes get weirder as the girl grows up, if not into wom-anhood, then into a girl for whom some man brings breakfast in bed.

Waldner's, Ryan's, Volkman's, and Jarnot's uses of rhyme are fore-grounded—they pop out—but they are also structural: rhyme occurs either at regular intervals, or very densely throughout the poem. Other fine recent uses of rhyme are irregular, scarcer within a given poem; rhyme works there as hexameters work within a pentameter norm (think of Pope's swift Camilla), or like sentence fragments in a poem made largely from complete grammatical units. Here is the end of Laura Kasischke's "Fashion Victim":

> Soon
> there will be nothing but obscurity
> as far as the eye can see. Until
>
> there's only one leaf left
> clinging to one tree. Until, like
>
> my father over there in his chair, my
> clothes are how you know it's me. (15)

Unless you count "obscurity," the rhyming words would not stand out absent the rhyme. Instead, the rhyme, and its irregularity, make the component words stand out: we are not likely to see these full rhymes coming, not even if we read down the end of each line. In the same way, we cannot learn to anticipate, much less predict, our own physical and mental decline. Kasischke does this sort of thing with sudden, irregular, full rhyme all the time. Its jaggedness, in her verse, emphasizes the unpredictability of even the stablest lives: as teenagers, as mothers, and as daughters (and almost all the people in Kasischke's poems act as one of those three), we ought to know that we can never know what comes next, cannot guess when past and present, syllable and syllable, will coincide.

If we ask why young-ish American poets, by and large, no longer use background rhyme—why most no longer even try to use it, even when they are trying to write in otherwise familiar, even traditional, modes—hypotheses are hard to test, but easy to come by. One hypothesis is simply that these poets (unlike, say, Wilbur) learned to read poetry generally by reading, first, the poems of modernism and after: they grew up with a norm that itself included many varieties of free verse. When you read Eliot, Williams, and Plath before you have read any Yeats or Pope or Browning—when you encounter the modernists, and their successors, first; when they produce your first ideas of what poetry is—rhyme may seem infinitely interesting (as it has to Kasischke, for example) but it cannot seem like a default form, like what poetry in general does. Centuries and even decades ago, many readers expect most kinds of poems to rhyme; those expectations affect what poets wrote, whether or not the poets chose to meet them. (Hart Crane may have been the first American poet to surprise his first readers— those in modernist little magazines—with obtrusive rhyme, foreground rhyme, against a free verse norm.) Now we expect that new poetry will not rhyme, and that expectation affects what we hear when it does. Foreground rhyme fits us, as background rhyme fit Pope's day; uses of rhyme in American English can take advantage of that unprecedented, and literally post-modernist, state of affairs. Rhyme can still be made useful, made to mean—and if it always stands out, it can even carry certain meanings more easily: it represents imposed (rather than discovered) order, artificial or fragile order, and irregular, fragmentary, temporary order at that.

It may also represent the past, a supposedly outmoded form of verse to match an earlier form of life, with its own more predictable (but not necessarily happier) rhythms and rituals. Indeed, the largely (though not entirely) disappointing territory of self-proclaimed U.S. New Formalist verse, which attempts to revive background rhyme for a world that has lost it, has shown a consistent (sometimes unintended) appeal to political conservatives who want to bring back earlier forms of social life too. Rhyme represents earlier forms of life for many American poets, and it stands out in part because it does so: that form of life may be earlier in ontogeny (childhood) as well as in history. In Kasischke's "Infants Corner" (the title refers to memorial stones for dead babies) it is both: Kasischke takes an otherwise unremarkable piece of epitaphic verse and relineates it to make recurrent but irregular foreground rhyme, a pattern that marks itself as contemporary (by contrast to the epitaph's regular meter). Reading the stones, Kasischke says,

> She
> liked the one that said, *Wipe*
> *your tears and weep no more, Little*
>
> *John has gone before*—so
> maudlin in its longing, like a drunk
>
> stumbling through a liquor store
> where they won't sell him any
> liquor anymore. (54)

What was once conventional seems "maudlin"; what was once consolation now seems like illusion, like a drunk's daily dose of alcohol.
The old epitaphic couplet does something, in this new context, but it
cannot do what it once did, just as the rhyme more-before does not
work the same way when it becomes an internal rhyme, and then rhymes
again with line-terminal "store" and with "anymore."

For Mary Jo Bang, in her latest book, the world of full rhyme is also
the world of Victorian childhood, of now-incredible consolations, on
which her own poems look back with a fascinated, appalled nostalgia.
Frequent foreground rhyme (both internal and line-terminal) presents
the forms and pleasures of the literary past and of the personal past (that
is, childhood) as if in a frame, in a museum, under glass, in a collectible
picture book, like the girl depicted in "And As In Alice," who holds a
stuffed bear:

> Who would dare hold a real bear so near the outer ear?
>
> She's wondering what possible harm might come to her
> If she fell all the way down the dark she's looking through.
> Would strange creatures sing songs
> Where odd syllables came to a sibilant end at the end. (6)

For Bang, rhyme itself ("odd syllables" that end alike) is what a girl hears
once she falls down a rabbit hole, into anachronistic fantasy. Rhyme
represents that fantasy, which we adults, we modern readers, have
outgrown—nonetheless, Bang suggests, we still want it: and she produces it—dare-bear, her, outer ear.

Rhyme means too old, incredible consolation; irregular foreground
rhyme describes that consolation, and our nostalgia for it, while saying
that we cannot have it. That is how "And Also for Alice" works, and it
is how rhyme works at greater length in Bang's "Mystery At Manor Close,"
whose title suggests (though it does not name) a Nancy Drew book:

> She makes a wish: that the Heather who left her
> In stormy weather will find herself
> In the mire of desires that cannot be easily realized.
> To your health, she says, and sticks out her foot

To feel the fire in its place. Here's to Bio-
In most of its many spheres. To the ear that hears
The clack of a gate latch. To the mouth and its legible
Little gray lies. To the brain with its hardwired fear.

And to cathexis, both far or near. Back at the manor,
There's mystery, a van and a driver, a girl's guide, a book.
The rescue of one in a basket about to be driven away by a crook. (36)

The fulfillment of line-terminal rhyme, like other sorts of fulfillment
(cathexis), can enter Bang's poems, but only as highlighted ironies, solutions to contrived or childish "mysteries"—the only kind that we can solve.
Background rhyme is a kept promise, a kind of reliability; Bang's intralinear chimes and unanticipated couplets are memorable without becoming reliable—there is nothing in adult life on which we should rely.

Bang uses full rhyme only when certain subjects solicit it, and she
usually attacks the sense of consolation it brings. Angie Estes, on the
other hand, uses foreground rhyme, along with rhyme-like euphonies,
consistently, and without trying to undermine the constructed order it
brings: her poems announce that they defend (as Merrill used to defend)
the aesthetic impulse in all its extravagance, all its attempts to hold off
the prose of the world. Here is the start of Estes's poem "Sans Serif":

It's the opposite of
Baroque so I want
none of it—clean
and spare, like Cassius
it has that lean
and hungry look, Mercury's
clipped heels, the rag
of the body without
breath. A chorus of
alleluias, on the other
hand, is not only opulent
but copious, a cornucopia
of opinion which concludes
that opera is work, the *haute* gold
opus of the soprano, which does not
oppress yet presses against
her chest . . . (*Chez Nous* 28)

Clean-lean, opposite-none of it, and then the flood of polysyllable near-rhymes in opulent-copious-cornucopia, oppress-press-chest, along with the full "rhymes" embedded in longer words: cornucopia, opus, soprano . . . Baroque indeed: so Estes defends herself against modernist claims for the clean, the realistic, the stripped-down. Such claims have been cases against rhyme *tout court* (in, for example, William Carlos Williams) but they have also been claims for background rhyme, contentions that honest verse patterns should work without ornament. For Estes neither claim is tenable. Human life is so hard that we should not have to read about it, nor to live it, "sans serif," and the human imagination is capacious enough that we need not. It is not a counsel of despair but a response to the memory of despair: we need artifice, or device, and we need (furthermore) to make an argument for the device, which we do (as the Russian Formalists used to say) by "baring the device," but with splendor, rather than Byronic irony, as a result.

Estes (who seems, to judge by her poems, to have grown up far from wealth, close to Appalachia) does not shirk the troublesome analogy between material wealth and the wealth of sound-patterns exemplified in her full rhyme: such rhyme is showy, and takes its place among her other showy effects. Consider the multiple, polyglot foreground rhyme in Estes's "Takeoff" ("Delilah" is the role in Camille Saint-Saëns's opera):

> Granted: a song is a verbal
> fence, and so Delilah sings *Mon coeur*
> *s'ouvre à ta voix*, *My heart opens*
> *at your voice*, but then must cut
> Samson's hair because he prefers
> God to her, Miss Taken
> For Granted. (*Tryst* 7)

Couer-hair-prefer-her: foreground rhyme here, both full and half- or off-rhyme, is so frequent that we might call it a structural principle, but it does not recur at regular intervals, nor at the ends of lines. Instead, it exists in a rich matrix of effects that also include other kinds of near repetition ("taken / for granite") and even rhymes that link the middle syllables of words:

> He meant to be
> diagonal like agony, to outlast
> the flat leaves of the hollyhock, which hasten
> to lace. (*Tryst* 8)

Estes uses foreground rhyme so densely and so often—it fits her purposes—because she wants to defend, and to highlight, artifice: life, her poems say, would scarcely be worth the pursuit if we could not celebrate what we have made of it, what skills make possible the forms of *poesis* that we pursue, in and outside poems. It is a Paterian, if not a Wildean, position, and she finds symbols for it, along with foreground rhymes, in palaces, in haute couture, in Appalachian basements, and in nonhuman nature too:

> if the sealed beaks
> of the swans could speak, they'd hear

> how the blue cornucopias
> of morning glory toot

> their own horns. (*Tryst* 17)

Beaks-speak, corn-morning-horn, perhaps even blue-toot: the rhymes and near-rhymes indeed "toot / their own horns," will not let us leave them alone.

I have distinguished two kinds of rhyme, foreground and background: some rhymes can belong to either class, depending on how we choose to hear the poem, but many rhymes are clearly one or the other. Background rhymes do not stand out when the poem is first heard, do not appear to drive the meaning, are not the most prominent sonic aspect of the poem, and are normally part of a regular recurring structure, compatible with the illusion of unpremeditated or conversational speech: we notice them (once we notice them) only when they occur at line-ends. Foreground rhymes stand out when the poem is first heard, may well appear to drive the meaning or otherwise highlight the arbitrariness, the constructedness, of the poem, because they "pop out": we notice them even when they occur irregularly, or within lines. Contemporary American poets who use rhyme very inventively usually use foreground rhyme, though their reasons for doing so are not always the same; all those reasons, however, highlight the fragility, the artificiality, or the nostalgic character of the order, and the consolation, we might seek in poems.

I do not want to claim more than the evidence shows. There are young and midcareer U.S. poets who use background rhyme well, (e.g. H. L. Hix, Christian Wiman, Melissa Range): when they do not sound almost imitatively close to Wilbur himself, they tend to use off-rhyme, quiet rhyme, conjunctions that earlier generations of poets who used rhyme at all (not just Victorians; Hart Crane, too, or Wilbur) would have thought out of bounds. Here is the start of a sonnet by Keetje Kuipers:

> At the minor league game where I blush for
> the teenage girl who trills our anthem through
> her nose and you eat three sausages, or
> four, without spilling on your perfect blue
> T-shirt, there are no reasons to be too
> unhappy, not with children who loudly
> beg for cotton candy or umpires who
> call out our favorite batter, or lastly
> the girl in green-rimmed glasses who sadly
> forgets to bring the beer. (61)

What would otherwise be full rhymes fall on unstressed line-terminal syllables (for-or), and on words ("through," for example) that would not otherwise bear much semantic weight: the rhymes and near-rhymes emerge gradually, as Graves said they should, from supposedly casual speech, so that a hasty reader might well miss them. Kuipers must work very hard to make the lines sound so colloquial, so conversational, the rhymes so muted, that they do not stand out, as none of the spectators at the game stand out: there are "no reasons to be too / unhappy," though there are no reasons for overt happiness as yet.

You can also hear background rhyme well used in Devin Johnston's recent verse. Johnston writes, not by coincidence, about what we can salvage from the past, what objects (he thinks like an archaeologist) might give us a non-ironic, non-reactionary, and yet a considered, a critical, relation to our various personal, environmental, and literary histories. In "Crows" Johnston imagines that the eponymous animals' calls connect the future to the distant past:

Their caw is not
for us, but calls
to corvid, canid
ringing out
tomorrow's *cras*
and love the dead. (26)

Again, this poet has had to work very hard, to use short vowels and muted half-rhyme, in order to create a stanza that counts even arguably as background rhyme. This first stanza rhymes axbaxb, the next two xcdxcd efgefg, comparing the crows' "wings and bills" to "initials from / the Book of Kells," another antique source (27). (*Cras* is what crows say in Latin.) Such serious and compact work with background rhyme remains rare among younger American poets of Johnston's intellect: it will be interesting to see how many, if any, follow his lead.

Works Cited

Texts quoted above but not listed among Works Cited *below may be found in* Representative Poetry Online, maintained by the University of Toronto under the general editorship of Ian Lancashire: http://rpo.library.utoronto.ca/display/

Auden, W. H. *The Dyer's Hand.* New York: Vintage, 1962. Print.
Bang, Mary Jo. *The Bride of E.* St. Paul: Graywolf, 2009. Print.
Creeley, Robert. *Collected Poems 1975-2005.* Berkeley: U of California P, 2008. Print.
Cushman, Stephen. *William Carlos Williams and the Meanings of Measure.* New Haven: Yale UP, 1982. Print.
Estes, Angie. *Tryst.* Oberlin, Ohio: Oberlin College P, 2009. Print.
Estes, Angie. *Chez Nous.* Oberlin, Ohio: Oberlin College P, 2005. Print.
Graves, Robert. *Collected Writings on Poetry, Volume One,* ed. Paul O'Prey. Manchester: Carcanet, 1995. Print.
Hamby, Barbara. *All Night Lingo Tango.* Pittsburgh: U of Pittsburgh P, 2009. Print.
Jarnot, Lisa. *Black Dog Songs.* Chicago: Flood, 2003. Print.
Johnston, Devin. *Sources.* New York: Turtle Point, 2009. Print.
Kasischke, Laura. *Lilies Without.* Keene, N.Y.: Ausable, 2007. Print.
Kasischke, Laura. *Fire & Flower.* Farmington, Maine: Alice James, 1998. Print.
Kuipers, Keetje. *Beautiful in the Mouth.* Rochester: BOA, 2010. Print.
Longenbach, James. *Modern Poetry After Modernism.* New York: Oxford UP, 1997. Print.

Merrill, James. *Collected Poems*, ed. J. D. McClatchy and Stephen Yenser. New York: Knopf, 2002. Print.

The New Princeton Encyclopedia of Poetry and Poetics, ed. Alex Preminger and T. V. F. Brogan. Princeton: Princeton UP, 1992. Print.

Ricks, Christopher, ed. *Joining Music With Reason: 34 Poets, British and American.* Chipping Norton, Oxfordshire: Waywiser, 2010. Print.

Ryan, Kay. *The Best of It: New and Selected Poems.* Boston: Grove/Atlantic, 2010.

Sorby, Angela. *Schoolroom Poets.* Lebanon, N.H.: U of New Hampshire P, 2005. Print.

Volkman, Karen. *Nomina.* Rochester: BOA, 2007. Print.

Waldner, Liz. *Trust.* Cleveland: Cleveland State University Poetry Center, 2009. Print.

Wilbur, Richard. *Collected Poems.* New York: Harcourt, 2004. Print.

I Am One of an Infinite Number of Monkeys Named Shakespeare, or; Why I Don't Own this Language

Benjamin Paloff

Have you ever heard a bad cover of one of your favorite songs? Did you declare—to yourself, to a friend, and perhaps a bit petulantly—that you prefer the original recording? Did you learn (later, on your own, if you were lucky; immediately, from that friend, if you were not) that the version you first came to love is actually the cover, and that the perceived interloper, still dripping with inadequacy, is the original?

This experience, whose universality only amplifies the sense of the uncanny we express when we ask, "Really? *That* one came first?"—also encompasses one of the key demands our critical readership makes on poetry. "Originality" is good; "inimitability" is better. I put these terms in quotation marks because I distrust them, and so have borrowed them from the thousands of book reviews that have used them in the last hundred years or more, rarely questioning what they mean or the hierarchy of value they imply. That is, when it comes to lyric expression, one strives to be the first, but one hopes to be the last as well, the alpha and the omega in one.

"Language, the mother of reason and revelation, its alpha and omega," Walter Benjamin quotes Johann Georg Hamann, the eighteenth-century mystical philosopher, in his posthumously published essay, "On Language as Such and on the Language of Man." But for Hamann, as for Benjamin, what is called "language" need not have anything to do with syntax, parts of speech, or speech at all. "For language is not a collection of discursive conventional signs for discursive concepts," Ernst Cassirer explains in *The Philosophy of Symbolic Forms,* "but is the symbol and counterpart of the same divine life which everywhere surrounds us visibly and invisibly, mysteriously yet revealingly. For Hamann as for Heraclitus, everything in it is at once expression and concealment, veiling and unveiling. All creation, nature as well as history, is nothing other than a message of the creator to the creature through the creature." And back to the Creator: as Benjamin puts it, "in naming the mental being of man communicates itself to God."

"Poetry"—Hamann again—"is the mother tongue of humankind." And so everything that there is to say is already here, in this world, waiting to be said, or said again, in a line of communication that merely reflects back to the Infinite that which the Infinite already contains. This point about originality, or the impossibility thereof, is hardly original. We hear it from the mouth of the Preacher in the Old Testament, which I like to read in the King James Version, if only because it is constantly reminding how little of my language, how little of what flows from my mouth or my keyboard and to which I might ascribe no origin before myself—how little of this begins or will end with me: "The thing that hath been, it is that which shall be; and that which is done is that which shall be done: and there is no new thing under the sun" (Eccles. 1:9). Poetry, lyric expression, is therefore not divine revelation, but a form of participation in a world that does not need our participation in order to keep on spinning. No, it is we who need to instantiate our connection to the world, and not the other way around. Thus Bruno Schulz, in a formula that reconfigures Hamann to emphasize our participation in making meaning over our claim to meaning as birthright, says, "Speech is the metaphysical organ of man."

At which point one of the editors of the present volume warns that all of these quotations at the beginning "occasionally felt a bit heavy." I feel it, too: when I am writing or speaking, the words of others, living and dead, weigh heavily upon me, and I want to make them invisible, except insofar as dropping one name or another might make me appear more attractive to the opposite sex and more imposing to my own— insofar as it might accentuate my originality. Otherwise, I might put Benjamin, Cassirer, and Schulz aside and pretend not only that the editor had said nothing, but that there had been no editors at all, and that I am not imagining you reading this, not imagining what you might be thinking as you read this, even as I am desperate for us to share this moment of reading. God forbid I should then quote Maurice Blanchot, who declares, with the absolute self-assurance which comes of being spot-on, that an essential feature of any conversation—perhaps *the* essential feature—is the silence in which nothing is said, and that the literary work exists only in "the intimacy between someone who writes it and someone who reads it." To call the written work and its creator "disposable" beyond this intimacy would be inaccurate, since the word itself suggests the *potential* for us to do without poems and their authors, whereas the disappearance of both, as well as of the reader, is already guaranteed, is in fact always already happening.

But who really wants to admit that poems, poets, and readers, that everything we say and do, could just as well not be said or done? Certainly not those who continue to cling to the traditional metaphor of the muse, which reverses the flow of communication, casting the message as a message from on high, and the poet as spiritual medium. If we adopt the position that poetry comes from somewhere beyond our experiential reality, and that it overcomes the poet, who then serves, perhaps even reluctantly, as its mouthpiece, then we cannot help but seek a one-to-one correspondence between the poetic text and the original it translates, or "carries across," from that ideal plane. And because this Saint Elsewhere is permanent and unchanging, poetry itself, if it's the real deal, if it's "inspired," is also everlasting. Thus Horace can rightly declare in the third book of his *Odes* that, through poetry, "I have raised myself a monument more lasting than bronze." And Alexander Pushkin, a true Romantic, can then out-Roman the Roman by announcing, "I have raised myself a monument not made by hands." Where Horace presses poetry into service as the guarantor of his historical legacy, for Pushkin the legacy is already due him, since he himself has faithfully served a higher spiritual power. Horace's *monumentum* becomes Pushkin's *pamiatnik*—from "*pamiat*," "memory"—and the comparison to bronze, which in Horace's former vocation as a soldier had been the principal instrument by which glory could be achieved, becomes something otherworldly, "not-made-by-hands," a religious term—*nerukotvornyi*—for an image of Christ that seems to materialize out of nowhere, as in the Edessa legend. What is so impressive about Pushkin's line, and more generally about the Romantic cult of inspiration, is how something so deliberately made, in a poem that takes Horace's line for its epigraph, can at the same time, in nearly the same words, lay claim to its own permanence and originality. This is Romantic irony at its most cunning.

In our own time, however, such claims rarely project the same irony. Most readers, it would seem, prefer to read a text that is unambiguously final, a preference that carries with it the macabre implication, never articulated aloud, that we also prefer our favorite poets dead, if only to prevent them from making subsequent alterations to the poems we love. One justification for this position follows what Galway Kinnell has called "the law of elapsed time," explaining (rather dubiously) that "revision succeeds in inverse ratio to the amount of time passed since the work was written." In other words, once the poem is written, revised, and settled, that should be it, since "the writer eventually loses track of what he or she was originally trying to do—or, more likely, was doing without trying." Another line of reasoning, one more obviously aligned with the prejudices of the New Criticism, questions whether we, as readers, have any right to read work that the author has not, as it were, "authorized" for general consumption. Such was Helen Vendler's displeasure in response to the 2006 release of Elizabeth Bishop's *Edgar Allen Poe and the Jukebox: Uncollected Poems, Drafts, and Fragments*, edited by Alice Quinn. At the time, Vendler argued not only that these were not "real poems," but that they were not "Elizabeth Bishop poems," that is, poems Bishop had sanctified with her name.

This insistence on keeping to one, final text and prizing its authenticity over other versions, whether prior or subsequent, is not merely a habit of reading, but is symptomatic of a common faith in the purity, the sanctity, of the "real poem." Though nearly every book of poems published in the United States today acknowledges that some of the poems printed therein first appeared elsewhere "in different forms" or "earlier versions," few readers are propelled from the book back to the journal, to the poem's former self. Fewer still—the scholar, the obsessed fan—dig into manuscript archives to find the earlier drafts, the notes, the letters to or from friends that contain the seeds of a beloved line, image, or idea. Of course, not everyone, even among the most ardent admirers of poetry, has the resources or inclination to perform this kind of sleuthing. But the very effort it demands is itself indicative of the fact that we regard those other texts as lesser precursors, mere shadows of the "authorized" or "definitive" edition, which is as close to the poem's singular ideal as we may ever hope to achieve.

Unless, on the other hand, the poem is something much more modest, what the Russian critic Vladislav Kulakov laconically describes as "a fact of language, its aesthetic dimension." Such an attitude demands that we accept the poem as product or trace, a verbal artifact of processes mental and physical, proactive and responsive, like any conversation, and like all things said in conversation ultimately destined for oblivion, though the conversation may go on. Here, the *poïesis,* or "making," of the poem is not its manifestation of a singular truth from Beyond. Rather, the poem is made from the materials at hand, which include the stuff of the author's own mind at work. "Language changes," Kulakov continues, "but new aesthetic possibilities depend not so much on material changes (lexical, functional) as on mental ones, what we might call an individual sense of language." To adopt this view is to accept that no version of a poem can claim primacy over any other. We may choose to focus our limited attention on a given draft (typically the "last"), but in any event the value our attention conveys originates with us, the readers, and not with the poem. "Whatever lies still uncarried from the abyss within / me as I die dies with me," reads the whole text of Frank Bidart's "Homo Faber." Yes, and sooner or later all the rest of it goes, too: the value we have assigned to the poem, the "we" who have assigned it, and in due course the poem as well.

Poetry in translation throws this issue into special relief, since for most of us the first translation of a poem we encounter is, for all practical purposes, the original. It therefore assumes an aura of inviolability. And yet, if it is a poem that attracts a lot of attention, violation is likely. It is a peculiarity of our literary culture that the appropriation and reworking of contemporaries' material that pervades our popular music through sampling meets such resistance when it comes to the written word. I do not wish to give the impression that anything goes; when it comes to demonstrable cases of plagiarism, I am admittedly merciless toward my students and sanctimonious before my friends. I nevertheless think it worth recognizing that even this "mercilessness" and "sanctimoniousness" guard a faith in the original, a fundamentally religious faith, and one whose need for defense belies its very claim to legitimacy.

Similarly, the vocabulary we have concocted to discuss the appropriation and rewriting inscribed in the very act of writing reflects our own uneasiness with what we might otherwise have to admit to be an incessant assault on originality, on the sanctity of the original text and, by extension, of its original author. Echo, allusion, adaptation, revision, paraphrase, transposition, translation, quotation—all of these terms and practices, and potentially many more, would seem to challenge the very notion of an original, if by "original" we mean an utterance that cannot have been, and that cannot be, said in any other way. The consummate expression of this challenge in the last half-century has been the already overtired practice of erasure, that is, the making of a new poem by scratching away lines, words, or parts of words from another text, which may be a forgotten older text (as in Mary Ruefle's *A Little White Shadow*) or as famous a poem as *Paradise Lost* (the basis for Ronald Johnson's *Radi Os*). Not only does the erasure suggest that there is another text behind the one previously presented to us, printed and bound, as "final." It evidences the likelihood that everything we read is already merely a draft of something that will follow it.

With the subversion of our faith in originality comes an attack on a more pervasive, though no less vague, critical cliché, that of the poet's "voice." Writers worth reading typically do have a distinctive way of using language, whether that distinctiveness obtains in their diction, central themes, navigation among semantic fields, range of reference, or style of reason. None of these things, however, nor the hundreds of other elements of rhetoric that we might add to the list, each of which provide a passage for our habitation of a text, is reducible to "voice." And if by that airy word we mean all of these distinctive features together, the *je ne sais quoi* that both accounts for our special attention to a particular poet and masks our reluctance to inquire past the surface of that attention, then the term's usefulness is all the more uncertain. And yet it is the reconstruction of the poet's voice in the new language that is so often cited as the translator's central task and, when that reconstruction falls short or to the side of our expectations, as the translator's failure.

This brings us to another remarkable implication of praise for "originality" and "inimitability": it generally refers to the poet, and not to the poem or poems that might be entered into evidence to support the claim. This makes such claims all the more suspect, if we are to take them seriously, since by claiming that So-and-So is an "original," nay, an "inimitable" poet, this originality is transferred automatically to the poems, *a priori,* before we've read them, before the poet has even written them. Here, too, what begins in mysticism ends in dogma. The poet, as the agent of an otherworldly power, produces work that cannot be rejected without also challenging that power.

When we first encounter this work in translation, however, we find a convenient way to avoid heresy. We simply blame the translator for any perceived inadequacy. The scribe errs of necessity, whereas the prophet cannot: this assumption lies at the foundation of the numerous beatitudes that axiomatize translation's failure. Long before the formula, attributed to Robert Frost, that "poetry is what is lost in translation," the Italian pun *traduttore-traditore* equated translation with treachery. A satirical column published in *The New York Times* in 1907 explains: " 'Traduttore traditore' (a translator is a traitor) is the neat phrase long ago applied by Italians to the French translators of Dante. Quite likely French politicians who, when they feel themselves undone, have had the habit of crying, 'We are betrayed!' will, with more appropriateness, in the future ejaculate, 'We are translated!' " The ejaculations of French politicians have in fact changed over the last hundred years, though in a way that would rather necessitate the translation of English into English.

"Every translation begins and ends in failure," Jean and Robert Hollander declare in the preface to their own recent translation of Dante. It is easy to understand why the translators of a given text might feel this way when surveying their own work. After all, for the literary translator—and the market dynamics of literary translation are such that very few translators are paid well enough to be motivated by anything but love—the text he or she is translating must, by definition, refer back to another text that has not only been previously encountered, but that also inspired enough admiration to demand many hours of lonely and frustrating labor over what might turn out to be, in the best case, a pretty decent cover of a favorite song.

But what pretext do other readers have to assume the original is a better, or even more authentic, experience than the translation? One who, upon reading Baudelaire's translations of Edgar Allen Poe, has been spurred to study English in order to read Poe in the original is unlikely, I think, to find his efforts rewarded. And while I have no Italian whatever, it is difficult for me to imagine that certain of Petrarch's sonnets can afford more pleasure in the original than Thomas Wyatt's versions have given me in English.

What these translations lack, of course, is the sacred aura of the original. That aura, however, is transferable, as we see every time we express admiration for a text we know only in translation. That Dante, who could not read Greek, knew Homer only from spotty translations did not prevent him from praising him among the ancients, in Robert Pinsky's version, as "their lord / The sovereign poet." Similarly, there is no shortage of essays in English devoted to the genius of Osip Mandelstam, though the authors of these appreciations rely most often on the small handful of poems translated by Clarence Brown and W. S. Merwin, versions that are remarkably unlike Mandelstam in both form and content. "Merwin has translated Mandelstam into Merwin," Brown notes in his introduction, which is inevitable, since the translator can only present to us what has resonated with his or her own sensibility.

Indeed, of the countless bromides that have accumulated around the question of translation's fidelity to the original—read: "fidelity," "original"—one that actually makes some sense belongs to Charles Simic. "Translation is an actor's medium," he explains. "If I cannot make myself believe that I'm writing the poem that I'm translating, no degree of aesthetic admiration for the work can help me."

What happens, then, when another actor assumes the role? Michael Hofmann, himself a veteran translator from German, illustrated this problem ruthlessly in a review of Zbigniew Herbert's *The Collected Poems*. The book consists of the work first published in 1967 as Herbert's *Selected Poems*, translated by Czesław Miłosz and Peter Dale Scott, and an enormous number of new translations by Alissa Valles; it does not include any of the versions done by John and Bogdana Carpenter, who until then had been Herbert's most productive proxies in English. At the beginning of his review, Hofmann notes: "I have the German translations and read them. I can't read Polish; but I have Herbert wherever I go. As I said in these pages a year or two back, he is the first poet I ever read. Probably he is as near to sacred to me as anything in or out of poetry is." He might as well stop there. For once a text is assigned sacred status, any effort to translate it, to say the same thing in other words, to interpret its meaning or intent, is heretical. (According to Louis Untermeyer, this was the oft-ignored second half of Frost's dictum, that poetry "is also what gets lost in interpretation.") And sure enough, Hofmann goes on to excoriate Valles for her shortcomings vis-à-vis the earlier Carpenter translations, through which Hofmann had gotten to know Herbert, or at least an important version of him. As Hofmann admits, he doesn't have access to the language in which Herbert composed his poems. If he had, he might have reconsidered many of his characterizations of Herbert's writing and his analysis of Valles' renderings, since much of what Hofmann has to say about Herbert is inaccurate, at least as far as the original Polish is concerned. Not that it matters: for Hofmann, as for most of us, some translations are effectively the original within the range of our own experience. All subsequent translations are mere imposters.

In fact, sacred texts—and here I mean those texts that are regarded as such by a religious community, though this could apply to Zbigniew

Herbert as well as to L. Ron Hubbard—are translations by definition: written, rewritten, transcribed, and redacted so many times that the human interventions that bring us the text, even one that we ourselves take for the word of God, are difficult or altogether impossible to reconstruct. Such is the case with the Old and New Testaments. The scribes' transcription of the Koran is an integral feature of its origin story, and the more fervently one believes that no deviations entered the text as it passed from God to the Prophet—and from the Prophet's lips to the scribes' pens, and from their pens to the codification produced by Uthman ibn Affan later in the seventh century—the more unambiguously such a text represents for that reader a translation of the original in the mind of God. And yet, paradoxically, each subsequent translation of the sacred text becomes an original for some reader, and as an original it must be defended against subsequent translation. Such was the case in the production of the Tyndale Bible (William Tyndale was burned at the stake in 1536) and the Matthew Bible (produced by John Rogers, a.k.a. "Thomas Matthew": the stake, 1555), though both were subsequently major sources for the King James Version, itself the fruit of several dozen translators' labors and now sacred to hundreds of millions. As Ma Ferguson, the first female governor of Texas, is reputed to have said, "If the King's English was good enough for Jesus Christ, it's good enough for the children of Texas!" (This would have been sometime in the twenties or thirties, but the earliest versions of this quip in the American press go back to the 1880s. Either everything is original, or nothing is.)

Though it is terminally flawed with respect to its reading of Herbert, Hofmann's review is a very effective inventory of Hofmann's reading of Hofmann reading Herbert. If this is a little cumbersome in its formulation, it is only because the process of encountering a poem—and, through the various displacements that we might call "translation," *re-encountering* it—is itself cumbersome, often in ways we do not wish to admit. And so we perform a radical simplification. It is all too easy to deride claims of sacredness, particularly when we do not share them, as a failure to perform the kinds of critical intervention that seasoned readers of literature perform all the time. But a fundamentalist reading—

one that takes the Book of Revelation not only as the word of John of Patmos, but as "the word of God, and of the testimony of Jesus Christ, and of all things that he saw" (Rev. 1:2), as well as a technically accurate manual on the structure of Creation—is a more radical intervention than anything that can be produced by the most sophisticated reader. For the fundamentalist inverts the relationship between representation and its object: he reverses the flow of communication, so that it is no longer man speaking to God, but the other way around. The text becomes an incontrovertible, self-evident reality, whereas the world itself is merely a shadow, an imperfect copy, an intermediary between the original (Paradise) and its return (the world after Judgment). Even more radically, the fundamentalist reader then claims never to have performed the intervention in the first place, since the origin of "the word of God" precedes anything the reader can take from it.

The notion of a sacred text as that which *cannot* be translated is nothing new, of course. In certain religious practices, as in Cabbalistic reading, the sacred text is not only a sequence of stories, parables, or laws, but an arrangement of figures originating in God and therefore a map of His creation. The figures cannot be "translated," because they cannot be moved without altering the map. The perfect poem, if we were to take this radical view to its logical extreme, would consist entirely of *hapax legomena*, words which not only appear just once in the poem, but which appear there and only there, in that single instance, and are therefore nearly impossible to define with any certainty. Or as Joseph Joubert jotted down in his notebook in 1797: "Sacred language. It should be hieroglyphical. All words should be hollowed out or in relief, chiseled or sculpted. Black and white, emptiness and fullness are suitable to it. Everything must be juxtaposed and united, but separated by intervals."

The evaluation of a translation's "faithfulness," while nearly universal as critical practice, is no less reflective of these radical assumptions. Initially, the term applied not to the correspondence between the original and its new version in another language, but rather to the faith—the belief, the worthiness in the eyes of God—of the man who produced it. "And surely how it hath happened," Thomas More remarks on the translation of the Bible into the vernacular in his *Dialogue Concerning Heresies*, itself a response to Tyndale's efforts at translation, "that in all this while God hath either not suffered, or not provided, that any good virtuous man hath had the mind in faithful wise to translate it, and thereupon the leastwise some one bishop, to approve it, this can I nothing tell . . ." Accordingly, the failure of a translated work to afford pleasure to the reader can now be attributed to the spiritual inadequacy of the translator relative to the sacredness of the original. Once again, when we find fault in a translated text and have no recourse to the original, we generally assume that fault rests with the translator, not the work translated. Hofmann's review of Herbert thus begins with an *ad hominem* attack on Valles, whose only crime is to have brought him news that he would rather not know, namely, that Herbert's work is not only what was already familiar to him through the Carpenters' translations, but something more as well. Which can only lead to spiritual doubt: if this poet, "as near to sacred to me as anything in or out of poetry is," might be in some way other than what one has known, then what else might he also be?

A lot. The power of a work over time derives in large part from the richness of its interpretive potential, its ability to provoke new responses, to confront us with unfinished emotional and intellectual business. In short, a really good poem keeps us coming back for more, not just for more of the same. Translation, like the discovery of earlier versions and manuscripts of a beloved poem, extends that potential considerably, not only by furnishing us with additional context and content, but by reminding us that we should not be so confident in our readings, that our sacred truths are far from settled. In this way, translations and alternate takes, even those we may deem inferior to the poems we carry around in our heads, suggest what Alice Fulton has called "a poetry of inconvenient knowledge." They tell us a truth about the world, about our world, that we would rather not know, namely, that we do not know this world as well as we would like to think. "Translation attains its full meaning in the realization that every evolved language (with the exception of the word of God) can be considered as a translation of all the others," Benjamin maintains. "Translation"—and here I would insist on adding poems, drafts, notes, and ultimately anything we might read or write with pleasure—"is removal from one language into another through a continuum of transformations." And this is why we need to keep saying more, assigning new names, changing our position, blaspheming against everything we hold sacred, remaining ever grateful for the time we have spent together.

Works Cited

Translations of Schulz, Pushkin, and Kulakov appearing in the text were done by the author.

Benjamin, Walter. "On Language as Such and on the Language of Man." *Reflections: Essays, Aphorisms, Autobiographical Writings.* Ed. Peter Demetz. Trans. Edmund Jephcott. New York: Schocken, 1978. 314-332. Print.

Bidart, Frank. *Desire.* New York: Farrar, 1997. Print.

Blanchot, Maurice. *The Space of Literature.* Trans. Ann Smock. Lincoln: U of Nebraska P, 1982. Print.

Brown, Clarence. Introduction. *The Selected Poems of Osip Mandelstam.* Trans. Clarence Brown and W. S. Merwin. New York: NYRB, 2004. Print.

Cassirer, Ernst. *Philosophy of Symbolic Forms, Volume 1: Language.* New Haven: Yale UP, 1955. Print.

Dante. *The Inferno of Dante.* Trans. Robert Pinsky. New York: Farrar, 1994. Print.

Fulton, Alice. *Feeling as a Foreign Language: The Good Strangeness of Poetry.* Minneapolis: Graywolf, 1999. Print.

Hofmann, Michael. "A Dead Necktie." *Poetry* May (2007): 117-129. Print.

Hollander, Robert, and Jean Hollander. Preface. *Inferno.* By Dante Aligheri. New York: Anchor, 2002. xiii-xv. Print.

Horace. *The Odes of Horace.* Trans. David Ferry. New York: Farrar, 1997. Print.

Johnson, Ronald. *Radi Os.* Chicago: Flood Editions, 2005. Originally published 1976. Print.

Joubert, Joseph. *The Notebooks of Joseph Joubert.* Trans. Paul Auster. New York: NYRB, 2005. Print.

Kinnell, Galway. Introduction. *The Essential Whitman.* Hopewell: Ecco, 1987. Print.

Kulakov, Vladislav. *Poeziia kak fakt.* Moscow: Novoe Literaturnoe Obozrenie, 1999. Print.

More, Thomas. *The Complete Works of St. Thomas More, Volume 6: A Dialogue Concerning Heresies.* Eds. Louis A. Schuster, Richard C. Marius, et al. New Haven: Yale UP, 1973. Print.

Ruefle, Mary. *A Little White Shadow.* Seattle: Wave, 2006. Print.

Schulz, Bruno. "Mityzacja rzeczywistości." *Opowiadania. Wybór esejów i listów.* Ed. Jerzy Jarzębski. Wrocław: Ossolineum, 1989. 365-368. A less precise translation of Schulz's essay appears in: *Letters and Drawings of Bruno Schulz.* Ed.

Jerzy Ficowski. Trans. Walter Arndt. New York: Fromm, 1988. 115-117. Print.

Simic, Charles. Introduction. *The Horse Has Six Legs: An Anthology of Serbian Poetry.* Minneapolis: Graywolf, 1992. Print.

"Traduttore Traditore." *New York Times* 10 June 1907: 6. Print.

Untermeyer, Louis. *Bygones: The Recollections of Louis Untermeyer.* New York: Harcourt, 1965. Print.

Vendler, Helen. "The Art of Losing." *New Republic* April 3 (2006): 33-36. Print.

Persona and the Mystical Poem

Elizabeth Robinson

In this essay, I will open a discussion on one of many possibilities for a contemporary poetry that embraces mysticism. By mysticism I mean an experience of presence or union that resists rational explanation; I do not find it necessary to make explicit a divinity or religious tradition or practice in this definition. A transcendent mystical experience, it would seem, is no longer available to the postmodern poet. Still, I have confidence in the great resourcefulness of poetry to find way: to query and then shape findings into a poetry that enters a terrain of experience that can't be accounted for by conventional logic.

Immediately, within this domain the problems of source and voice arise: what is the source of poetry and how does it find voice? If an individual poet articulates a purportedly mystical vision or experience, how does the limitation and partiality of that voice mediate mystical "information"? From the outset, let me acknowledge that the issue of "source" can't be resolved. It is a marker of the value of poetic practice that such irresolution is a spur to poetry's ongoing exploration rather than an obstacle to it. Yet where there is no stable originary site, the poem itself becomes a site, *the* site, animated by curiosity, and perhaps even wonder. Ann Lauterbach gets at the heart of my concern and commitment when she asserts that the poem makes a claim, as if "you could write *away from* and *into* simultaneously, so that the temporal articulates only presence" (13).

Presence, as itchy as that word is, provides, in my estimation, the most enduring value of poetry. Correspondingly, that poetry can register many sorts of presence is a sign of its hardiness. A healthy art will beguile multiple voices without undue consternation that their discrete origins can't be clearly traced. Thus I'll turn to a consideration of persona as concurrently invocation and mediation of the mystical. It's long been a poetic truism that the poet is a conduit for the muse or for the spirit. My investigation here will consider the ways modern and contemporary poets have deliberately cultivated other voices and/or personae as a means of invoking, cultivating, or creating presence. Writing within the guise of a persona may be intrinsic to writing itself, as Rimbaud's "I is an other" reminds us. Nevertheless, personae offer the poet powerful tools into the speculative, multivocal authority of the poem's more uncanny movements.

The nature of presence in poetry and mystical utterance is fraught. How can the distinct textures of an author's voice be relevant if that speaker is only a vehicle for utterance that originates in unmapped sites? It's easy to suspect that the author is self-aggrandizing, claiming authority that has been swiped from a source whose legitimacy cannot be checked or is inarguable. Anne Carson addresses exactly this problem in part four of her essay "Decreation," when she observes the contradiction between mystic women writers insisting that mystical experience hinges upon the erasure, even annihilation of the self, while at the same time partaking of "the brilliant self-assertiveness of the writerly project . . . the project of telling the world the truth about God, love and reality" (171). Carson says flatly that this inconsistency cannot be resolved because to be a writer is to "construct a big, loud, shiny centre of self from which the writing is given voice and any claim to be intent on annihilating this self while still continuing to write. Giving voice to writing must involve the writer in some important act of subterfuge or contradiction" (171).

Yet this articulation seems a fundamental misunderstanding of the operations of art and faith. As theologian Amy Hollywood notes, such mystical occurrences do "mark the limits of experience yet seem to require some lingering subjectivity (the body that reacts?) if that dissolution is to be lived and communicated" (57). Inside the struggle for vision and understanding, we can, like Jack Spicer, "worship / These cold eternals for their support of / What is absolutely temporary" (26). Carson's stance, while initially seeming reasonable, entails a fundamental misreading of mystical experience. The "big, loud, shiny centre of self" from which writing is given voice can be understood as a mirror, and a distorted one at that. In poetry and mystical utterance, there is no necessary disagreement between the simultaneity of the speaker's voice and the voice that arrives from outside. Jack Spicer, whose poetry demonstrates a fascination with persona, address, and source, continually calls upon the figures of the mirror and of the ghost as a means by which the reflective and haunting functions of poetry are not merely reiterations of the self, but revelatory sites of deformation. In a letter to his friend Joe, included amid the poems of "Admonitions," Spicer asks about the poems, "Are they anything better than a kind of mirror?" He goes on to respond to his own question:

> In themselves, no. Each one of them is a mirror, dedicated to the person that I particularly want to look into it. But mirrors can be arranged. The frightening hall of mirrors in a fun house is universal beyond each particular reflection. . . . Mirror makers know the secret—one does not make a mirror to resemble a person, one brings a person to the mirror. (157)

The implication of this image is that the mirror can demonstrate to the self an other, unfamiliar self, a nod of recognition that reflects in excess of known presence.

Indeed, in "Heads of the Town," Spicer, playing off of Cocteau's film version of the Orpheus story says flatly, "Cocteau invented mirrors as things to move through. I invent mirrors as obstacles" (285). This statement establishes two things. First, Spicer is using the mirror specifically to *deny* its transparency as reflecting a true image back at the viewer. Second, the mirror *thwarts*. It is not a portal but blockade that makes evident an insuperable separation: "The edges of a mirror have their own song to sing. The thickness seems alien to The Poet and he equates his own hell with what is between them" (276). Seen this way, the mystic experience is a harsh inversion of what Carson describes. The authority of the poet's voice is beholden to its own absolute limitation. The voice of the poet effects separation from the very source of light that enables the mirror, in the first place, to reflect an image.

The brassiness of any articulation is merely a reflection bounced off another or prior source; it is not a puffed up iteration of the self. This struggle to evade the habituated tics of selfhood in the service of some larger purpose is everywhere evident in Spicer's poetry. Note the way he stretches poetics in the epistolary exchanges and poems of "After Lorca." Here Spicer enters into correspondence with (a safely dead) Lorca. Not only does he animate Lorca's voice by having the deceased (and reluctant) poet write an introduction to a series of Spicer's so-called translations of Lorca's poems, he engages Lorca in correspondence (both literally and figuratively). The aforementioned translations are deliberate disruptions of Lorca's work. This catalyzes an assault on authorial voice that is playful, distorting, and also deeply earnest. As Lorca ruefully notes in the introduction,

> Mr. Spicer seems to derive pleasure in inserting or substituting one or two words which completely change the mood and often the meaning of the poem as I had written it. More often he takes one of my poems and adjoins to half of it another half of his own, giving rather the effect of an unwilling centaur. (Modesty forbids me to speculate which end of the animal is mine.) Finally there are an almost equal number of poems that I did not write at all . . . and I have further complicated the problem . . . by sending Mr. Spicer several poems written after my death. (107)

The poetics here might not be overtly mystical (though the arrival of posthumously written poems suggests something mysterious is afoot!), but they most definitely play with authorship as a conduit of information or expression that cannot be readily controlled or confined. Spicer audaciously claims the authority of conversing not only with a famous poet, but with a famous *dead* poet. This may seem exactly the kind of self-aggrandizing gesture Anne Carson objects to: a contradiction of the self-erasure which would seem to legitimate the poet's/mystic's claim to mediate the transcendent. Yet Spicer brilliantly shows that it is exactly the adoption of persona(e) that enacts juxtapositions that relativize all individual selfhood(s) as transitory and mutable within their need to express (or at least point toward) some other form of duration and meaning.

In fact, in his letters to a deceased Lorca, Spicer insists, "It is precisely because these letters are unnecessary that they must be written" (110). However, Spicer's writing is not flippant, nor is it a leap into poetic play that disregards history. Rather, Spicer's affinity for Lorca is poignant as Spicer plumbs the lineage that is most meaningful to him, a Spicerean *duende* if you will. By claiming this tradition and playing out its ramifications, Spicer hones continuities. At the same time, variations flourish and bring texture to ongoing themes and threads. In other words, the layered repetitions of tradition, even of mystical tradition, result in "generations of different poets in different countries patiently telling the same story, writing the same poem, gaining and losing something with each transformation—but, of course, never really losing anything" (111).

"Invention," Spicer elaborates, "is merely the enemy of poetry" because while prose invents, "poetry discloses" (111). The role of the poet is therefore not to adorn language with newness and invention, but to strip it down to the place where, however strangely or idiosyncratically, poetry hollows out, reveals, the space of presence that we would otherwise assume as absence. This disclosure reveals what? It is not poetry or mystic utterance defining itself, but a strangely apophatic use of language. Just as a persona puts on the mask of identity, it troubles and undoes identity. Spicer is not Lorca; he and we know this, delightedly, all through their correspondence and through Spicer's translations. The eeriness of disclosure here has to do with Spicer's drive to locate the real. But his is a reality that is not to be apprehended through conventional, material measures. Spicer ultimately says good-bye to a ghost who "occasionally looked through my eyes and whispered to me . . . but [who is] now achieving a different level of reality by being missing" (153). Through his play with persona, Spicer has established the reality of presence that is most manifest in traces that can't be tracked back to stable identity or origin.

Spicer will come back to this matter again and again. Later in "Fifteen False Propositions Against God," Spicer avers "The self is no longer real / It is not like loneliness / This big huge loneliness. Sacrificing / All of the people with it" (195). The selfhood of the writer achieves a felicitous irrelevance. Selfhood is, in fact, metaphoric. In its reflective agency, it oscillates continually between "isness" and "is-notness." Note how Spicer uses the second person pronoun "you" in a poem from "Homage to Creeley" in what is apparently direct address, but ends by adding, "For example / the poem does not know / Who you refers to" (255). A page later in the same sequence, he elaborates the metaphoric-metaphysic continuum:

> On the mere physical level
> There is a conflict between what is and what isn't
> What is, I guess, is big
> And what isn't, bigger
> Metaphysically speaking
> What aren't casts no shadow
> And what are is bigger than the moon, I guess,
> Bigger than that boy's pants. (256)

Lest the reader retain any confusion as to whether the self is essentially a channel for the writer, a vehicle that conveys "other" knowledge (or the very lack thereof), we can consider one of Spicer's other favorite conductive images: that of the ghost. The ghost is the persona par excellence in Spicer's work because it doesn't represent identity *per se*. Rather the ghost is the aftereffect or presaging of identity without ever requiring the robustness of identity one would typically know as presence. At the beginning of "Homage to Creeley," the narrator of the so-called "explanatory notes" notifies the reader, "I am the ghost of answering questions. Beware me. Keep me at a distance as I keep you at a distance" (249). The information here is anything but illuminating. The ghost is not biddable. It is dangerous and untrustworthy. It is best to stay at a distance.

Later in the poem, the reader gains a little insight in the nature of ghosts: "They are frightened and do not know what they are, but they can go where the rabbits cannot go. All the way to the heart" (268). On the following page, Spicer lists three ghosts and asks, "Can you imagine ghosts like that translating these poems into / New English?" (269). Tellingly, these frightened entities whom Spicer considers with mild derision, are in the odd position of making translations, much as Spicer did in his "translations" of Lorca. The poem lapses thereafter into lists of pronouns, still further disrupting the idea of identity and the authority of the voice. In the accompanying "explanatory note," Spicer writes, "The three ghosts have names that are mockeries of your names. Your names (and theirs) are the afterwards mentioned pronouns" (269).

Ghosts function in much the same way that mirrors do in Spicer's poems and this parallelism is a fascinating reconception of mystic expression within the poem. Like the mirror, the ghost cannot offer a stable image or character to the viewer. The ghost is by nature bereft of its former living self, and so thwarts the discrete "truth" of personhood. As a poetic trope, the ghost forces distance between the gaze or ear and the image or song of the poem. Spicer's writing is assertive; it has a certain bravado that would seem to assert authorship, and yet this is play on the surface of the poem, an irony that points to the deeper object of his poetics. The poems are, in effect, *translations* and they openly display their flaws and inaccuracies. In so doing, they point to what isn't there. The speaker may boast his presence as creator of, or voice within, the poem, but this identity is little more than a "mockery of your name" that crumbles into the weak, proliferating, and featureless pronoun.

Akin to this, Simone Weil's aspiration was that she could efface herself so fully that the unadulterated presence of God could move more directly through her: "The self is only the shadow which sin and error cast by stopping the light of God, and I take this shadow for a being" (35). Here recurs the problem Carson raised concerning the relative loudness of the authorial voice in relation to the divinity for which it purports to speak. Note, however, Weil's comment on decreation, where she says, "Being does not belong to man [*sic*], only having. [. . .] What he can know of himself is only what is lent to him" (33). Seen this way, any word or utterance is a borrowing from larger meaning, and as such it marks its own partiality and limitation. Writing about the Jewish-Catholic philosopher Edith Stein, Fanny Howe clarifies this paradox; Howe elucidates that the speaking "I" is essentially exploratory, even playful, and creatively irresolute. Noting that Stein's formal academic writing is turgid and airless, Howe asks:

> Is this just because the first person—her "I"—had been banished from the essay as being an inappropriate guest at the table of ideas? Closing the grammatical system off from the presence of the writer is often a

way of banishing bewilderment from the prose. The "I" is a wild card that someone with her training does not allow in the deck. It undermines the overdetermined. To be a questing presence in her own written sentence would be a symptom of uncertainty and would thereby undermine the whole system she was defending. (46)

Similarly, in his "Palimpsest" chapter in *The H.D. Book*, Robert Duncan offers a discussion of the relation of voice and palimpsest. Duncan's reading here is initially of H.D.'s novel *Palimpsest*, but he broadens his discussion to consider the palimpsest itself, a parchment whose text has been overwritten with another text. Duncan sees the palimpsest as an apt metaphor for persona, noting that an image "from which one writing has been erased to make room for another may also be the image of an identity where one person has been erased to make room for another, a life or lives erased to make room for another life" (101). In Duncan's reading, use of personae has the quality both of reincarnation and access to a collective imagination. Both of these readings hazard the possibility of a totalizing vision in which all imaginations or lives are linked in a comprehensive system. This kind of system needn't be posited for mystical experience to be valid. I prefer the resonance of a passage found later in Duncan's essay, and which I'll cite at length. What he says about H.D.'s novel is applicable to the import of persona more broadly:

> Language becomes throughout a ground of suggestion and association, a magic ground, a weaving of phrases echoing in other phrases, a maze of sentences to bind us in its spell, so that we begin to be infected with the sense of other meanings and realms within those presented. . . . We must come back and back to the same place and find it subtly altered in each return, like a traveler bewildered by lords of the fairy, until he is filled with a presence he would not otherwise have admitted. Here it is not past time or present time but the blur, the erasure itself, that is the magic ground in which an image may occur. (109)

Most tellingly, Duncan helps us to understand that the author or speaker does not claim ultimate authority, but rather the author is the one who "must read the message the Presence presents" (121).

This exalted form of "reading" is beautifully exemplified in the poetry of Jean Grosjean. Grosjean, who was for a time a Catholic priest, takes on the personae of various biblical characters in several of the sequences in *An Earth of Time* (translated from the French by Keith Waldrop). In these poems, Grosjean continually pulls at the fabric and nature of "voice," standing both within and outside the character for whom a given poem is named. In addition, these poems often address a "you" who is both reader and, apparently, God. In this way, the poems compel the participation of numerous voices while simultaneously ruffling the possibility of direct address or constant identity. Situating the speaker of "Job 1" in an environment "where my mirages huddle," Grosjean has Job mark his own contingency, not merely as one who will suffer arbitrarily, but as one whose very identity is up for grabs:

> My room burns itself out in your creating presence. Nothing's to wait for, your gifts being only your love's momentary face. In your presence, anyone's bound to be preposterous. (69)

The poem establishes from the outset that it will not be a conventional retelling of the Job story, and its mischievous irony warns us that in the approach to the Divine—to the unknown—any claim to identity or persona is absurd. This lightness of touch infuses the whole sequence, as when the speaker reproaches God for abandoning him, observing, "You were never, talkative magpie, entirely there," and conjuring the striking image of a "ghostwriter's dentures punctuating the universe" (71). This lively dialogue presses upon the ephemerality of the would-be conversation partners. Grosjean's perceptions are so arresting that it takes a while before the reader absorbs the unease caused by the unsteadiness of identity and address here.

In "Job 2," the poem takes a further turn. Opening with a rebuke to the "Father," the first paragraph ends, "Still, I alone can teach you to expect no return. Heads of mountains collide with clouds" (70). The dialogue is truncated as the speaker teaches the *reader* that there can be no return, no reciprocity. This is an unexpected inversion, for the structure of the poem has thus far been that God-reader is the silent interlocutor who takes in author-speaker-Job's reflections. God holds the power and seems merely to absorb Job's outcry until this sudden overturning of authority. Here, it is *Job* who is resituated as the absent presence, saying in the next paragraph, "I leave you only my absence to despise. The most delectable pipeful that ever I've puffed" (70). Here indeed the reader, recalling Duncan's statement, may read the message the Presence presents: it transpires on a teetering ground where presence exchanges itself for absence, one speaker for another, and the reader's authority and distance are probed by the agency of the poem. The soft irony of the poem presses on to deeper questioning, and the story of Job is renewed for us.

When Grosjean moves next into sincere lament, the merging of personae, of Job and of God, is moving: "from behind the pain asleep in my mouth you cast your light" (71). The quality of language shifts subtly from the bounce of metaphor to a more affective, imagistic tonality: a muted voice within a voice. By the final section of the poem, the voice of Job and his God are so intertwined that the reader reads them properly as one, "Last time, you no longer spoke. Everything that was to come, suddenly undone," the speaker says, and adds, "I remember that time and how, playing my own role, I had memorized almost all the others" (73). Presence here frays: "I shall weave from your lackluster lips a garment to wear through the rain" (73). The poem's ensuing insights collapse identity, bringing Job and God together in their lament, a distorted and yet mystical union. There is no divine, no mortal, no reader or read, but only "Empty bottle." Personae here are finally distilled so that the reach beyond individual identity diffuses into erasure: "to be so little there that you will be there alone" (73).

Grosjean has reanimated an archetypical character with a convincing modern voice. He inhabits Job, and the heuristic reach of this "reading" rereads the divine as well. Here one can see that those who disdain the lyric "I" for its presumptuous, epiphanic point of view haven't properly considered the ways that locating the movement of a poem within a persona can stretch and dislocate that "I" in surprising, refreshing ways. Ann Lauterbach sums this up at the close of her essay, "Is I Another?" when she asserts:

> The idea of "objective uncertainty" is, in my view, a key to postmodern poetics. If the "I" finds its way out of the egotistical sublime and toward the alterity implied by all imaginative acts, then it will once again initiate paths away from self-absorbed narcissism to a recognition of the linguistic matrix that binds us to each other and to the world. (39)

A writing practice that rejects absolutes and which is generally not deistic properly problematizes the idea of reception from some privileged site of knowledge. A prophetic poetry that tries to rise above historical context almost immediately begins to deconstruct itself. And a voice that would claim transtemporal consistency is likely to lose authority rather than convince readers of its legitimacy. These are all problems over which a contemporary writer stumbles when she approaches poetry as potentially mystical. Yet the curiosity that undergirds the agency of mystical writing is recurrent and persistent. How, then, to trace or measure presences that resist any conventional circumscription? How does the writer express ideas that she is conscious are "not her own"?

Here I concur with Robert Duncan that our "experience of form throughout is a faith in the voice's telling that we follow" (122). To follow is, I emphasize, not to *know*. Yet a poetry that can admit the possibility of the mystical, specifically via the mediation of personae, opens the way to a poetry that creates its own transcendence without ceasing to follow, and without forcing the poem into the limits of individual knowing. A poetics of personae permits the speaker to speak in many, even contradictory, voices, testing attention and perception against what Simone Weil called "experimental certainties." The purpose of such poetry is not to achieve a state of ultimacy, but to keep desire and curiosity aloft. The poem's great service to us, its readers and writers—its personae— might well be to remind us, as Barbara Guest wrote, that "no matter what there is on the written page something appears to be in *back of everything that is said, a little ghost*" (100). The mystical poem is not a poem of completion and resolution. It is a poem of gesture and remainder. It is a poem of one voice and then another.

Works Cited

Carson, Anne. *Decreation*. New York: Vantage, 2005. Print.

Duncan, Robert. *The H.D. Book: The Collected Writings of Robert Duncan*. Berkeley: U of California P, 2011. Print.

Grosjean, Jean. *An Earth of Time*. Trans. Keith Waldrop. Providence: Burning Deck, 2006. Print.

Guest, Barbara. *Forces of Imagination*. Berkeley: Kelsey St., 2003. Print.

Hollywood, Amy. *Sensible Ecstasy*. Chicago: U of Chicago P, 2002. Print.

Howe, Fanny. *The Wedding Dress*. Berkeley: U of California P, 2003. Print.

Lauterbach, Ann. *The Night Sky*. New York: Viking, 2005. Print.

Spicer, Jack. *My Vocabulary Did This to Me*. Ed. Peter Gizzi and Kevin Killian. Middleton: Wesleyan UP, 2008. Print.

Weil, Simone. *Gravity and Grace*. London: Routledge, 1992. Print.

A Wilderness of Monkeys

David Kirby

> Tell a little & he is Hamlet; tell all & he is nothing. Nothing has life
> except the incomplete.
> —KEATS

> A portrait is a likeness in which there is something wrong about the
> mouth.
> —JOHN SINGER SARGENT

At Once Starkly Simple and Endlessly Ambivalent

The most beautiful sentence in the English language consists of the thirty-nine words that open "The Fall of the House of Usher": "During the whole of a dull, dark, and soundless day in the autumn of the year, when the clouds hung oppressively low in the heavens, I had been passing alone, on horseback, through a singularly dreary tract of country." What is it about this sentence that charms so? Surely it is not the hard road the traveler is following but the prospect of respite, for we have all passed through dreary tracts to some place of warmth and cheer, and that place has been all the warmer and cheerier for the dreariness that preceded it.

Yet notice how indistinct Poe's words are. From the moment we first put pencil to paper, we are told to use concrete imagery. But Poe's images are hardly worthy of the name. Neither the man nor the horse is described, not the land they pass over nor the sky above them. Yet we are drawn in: clip, clop we go on the way to our reward. It'll be a good one, but we can't see it, because it lies just outside the margin of the page.

Even more than fiction, songs rely on indistinctness. When Johnny Cash sings (in "I Still Miss Someone")

At my door the leaves are falling
A cold dark wind has come
Sweethearts walk by together
And I still miss someone,

who does not see the lonely man looking out on an autumn evening, the light almost gone from the sky as lovers hurry by arm in arm, the leaves crunching under their feet as they hurry off to dinner or a party or a bed as he sees in the shadows the half-forgotten face and figure of someone he can barely stand to think of, someone whose name he can't utter for fear of the pain its utterance will bring, pain he can only hint at? Yet Cash paints his picture so well that, for a moment, we, too, are that man. As in the Poe story, something better awaits us, and it will please us more because we spent a few moments in the sad man's shoes.

Here's a third example of indistinctness, this one from *The Iliad*. When Achilles says, "Fat sheep and oxen you can steal; cooking pots and golden-maned horses you can buy; but once it has left the circle of his teeth, the life of a man can be neither replaced, nor stolen, nor bought." The circle of his teeth: you can't but see not only a skull or a dental chart, possibly your last set of x-rays, but also a figure on his death bed, maybe a warrior on the plains of Troy or an elderly relative or even yourself, just as you can't not hear the rattling sigh of the last breath as it leaves the body.

Recently I heard a poet read a poem about his mother, who had died a few years before, and as a preface, he said that he dreamt his mother was telling "other dead people" about the first time he had sex. In the poem itself, he put flesh on his mother and the sex act itself, but the phrase that stuck with me throughout the reading was "other dead people": you see them instantly, faceless yet shrouded in their burial garments, motionless yet menacing.

And one more example of indistinctness before a few words of explanation. In *Something in the Air: Radio, Rock, and the Revolution That Shaped a Generation*, Marc Fisher notes that "Radio lends itself to nostalgia, to a pining for the innocence of a summer's night listening to baseball from a far-off city, the signal fading in and out, the crack of the bat sometimes lost in the sizzle of static from a distant lightning bolt." You're not told about the farm kid, the quiet bedroom, the house where Mom and Dad are winding down the day and getting ready for the next one, the dogs settling down under the porch and the larger animals asleep in the barn, and, in the distance, the little town with its single stoplight, its one drug store and barber shop. But you don't need that information: you have it already.

In *What Good Are The Arts?*, John Carey argues that one of great literature's chief virtues is indistinctness, as when Shylock speaks of "a wilderness of monkeys" or Caliban of the "noises, / Sounds, and sweet airs" that fill the isle or Macbeth of the "Good things of day" versus "night's black agents."

And in *Will in the World: How Shakespeare Became Shakespeare*, Stephen Greenblatt says *Hamlet* was a breakthrough for Shakespeare because, whereas he'd written tragedies before, here he used

> a new technique of radical excision. . . . Shakespeare found that he could immeasurably deepen the effect of his plays, that he could provoke in the audience and in himself a peculiarly passionate intensity of response, if he took out a key explanatory element, thereby occluding the rationale, motivation, or ethical principle that accounted for the action that was to unfold. The principle was not the making of a riddle to be solved, but the creation of a strategic opacity. This opacity, Shakespeare found, released an enormous energy that had been at least partially blocked or contained by familiar, reassuring explanations.

So we don't know why Hamlet behaves the way he does, just as we don't know why Iago hates Othello so much or Lear and Cordelia behave so perversely. But this indistinctness lures as Poe's opening sentence or Johnny Cash's lines do. We lean into the work; we want to know more.

Yet indistinctness predates Shakespeare considerably. Ann Marlow writes in *How to Stop Time: Heroin from A to Z* that:

> Because my father read to me from a huge illustrated book of Greek myths at my bedtime, I was immersed in the world of ancient Greece. Friends are surprised to hear that I enjoyed them, but these mysterious legends, whose meanings are at once starkly simple and endlessly ambivalent, are well suited to a child's mind. Children share the cruelty and intolerance of Greece, as well as its closeness to magic and the unconsciousness.

Ambivalence always sounds like a bad thing when somebody's nagging you to make up your mind. But what's wrong with taking your time?

What's wrong with thinking a lot about a poem or a scene or a character? What's wrong with thinking about it forever?

And don't forget the "gaps" or "blanks" Wolfgang Iser praises in *The Act of Reading*. The great works are asymmetrical, says Iser, and it is you and I who provide the symmetry. Or not. But no one's going to read a work or watch a movie or look at a painting that is clear, distinct, symmetrical. Indeed, who would want to?

"A man is a god in ruins," says Duke Ellington, and the artist's job is make that person a god again.

One Foot on the Platform

Nowhere is the power of indistinctness more apparent than in music. When Peggy Lee's "Is That All There Is?" became a runaway hit, no one could figure out if Jerry Leiber and Mike Stoller's Kurt Weill-ish music and lyrics signaled jubilation or despair. "If that's all there is, my friends / Then let's keep dancing / Let's break out the booze and have a ball."

And when the language is even less distinct—when it's nonsense—the effect can be even greater. Producer Cosimo Matassa is responsible for some of the liveliest pop music of the mid-twentieth century, and the songs that came out of Cosimo Matassa's studio on the corner of Dauphine and Rampart Streets in New Orleans are, for the most part, what Matassa calls "celebration songs." In a 2007 *Offbeat* interview, he tells Todd Mouton that while songs like Little Richard's "Tutti Frutti" as well as Huey "Piano" Smith & The Clowns' "Don't You Just Know It," Jessie Hill's "Ooh Poo Pah Doo," and Sugar Boy Crawford's "Jock-A-Mo" feature phonetic vocalizations some might call nonsense lyrics, in each case the artist is using his own language to express the simple pleasures of living.

"You can imagine children or adults dancing and skipping, finger-popping," says Matassa. "All of 'em move—that's the central thing with all of those songs. Some of 'em are totally child-like, but they were expressions of joy. These were expressions of emotion; you can't reject those. They get too analytical about the records. And most stuff isn't that cerebral—it's visceral."

Is the same not true in poetry, from Lewis Carroll's "the slithy toves / Did gyre and gimble in the wabe" to Emily Dickinson's "The doom's electric moccasin" and "Like rain it sounded till it curved"? And what about her "Diadems—drop—and Doges—surrender— / Soundless as dots—on a Disc of Snow—."

Feminist critic Ellen Willis writes in *Beginning to See the Light: Sex, Hope, and Rock-and-Roll* that she suspends her feminism when the Stones' "Under My Thumb" comes on at a party. Everybody wants to dance, and everybody wants to get somebody under their thumb.

Ann Marlow again:

Rock is about not having enough time to think or find your bearings, certainly not enough time to procrastinate or rationalize. This is one major reason it's been condemned as mindless music, assuming the equivalence of the superego and mindfulness. But Western philosophy began in haste, with the simulation of rapid-fire argument in the dialogues of Plato I spent so much time analyzing in college and grad school. And most of the philosophical writing I like shares with rock qualities of brevity, speed, and directness. Descartes, Wittgenstein, Nietzsche, Adorno, and Plato were never easy, and rarely unambiguous, but they went straight to the point. They have a quality of motion shared by every great rock song.

And here's how Pete Townsend of the Who (quoted by Greil Marcus in *Lipstick Traces: A Secret History of the Twentieth Century*) characterizes the power of rock 'n' roll:

Mother has just fallen down the stairs, dad's lost all his money at the dog track, the baby's got TB. In comes the kid with his transistor radio, grooving to Chuck Berry. He doesn't give a shit about mom falling down the stairs. . . . It's a good thing you've got a machine, a radio that puts out rock and roll songs and it makes you groove through the day. *That's the game, of course: when you are listening to a rock and roll song the way you listen to 'Jumpin' Jack Flash,' or something similar, that's the way you should really spend your whole life.* [Emphasis mine.]

So music, like stories and poems and myths, thrives on indistinctness. And the best kind of indistinctness is that which promises some wonderful thing to come: a haven in a desolate world, a sweetheart in a lonely one, a life that begins as a cross-fire hurricane and ends as a gas! gas! gas!

There is a tipping point in art, often a wet-eyed moment in which a trainload of sorrow is on the verge of breaking through. Consider a song made famous by the Drifters, "Save the Last Dance for Me" by Doc Pomus. Born Jerome Felder, Doc Pomus was, in addition to being a supremely talented songwriter, a homely, overweight cripple. One of his most memorable songs comes from Doc's memory of his wedding day, as he sat with his crutches and watched his brother Raoul whirl the new bride around the floor. Now imagine the recording session: Ahmet Ertegun is producing the song for the Drifters, and just before lead singer Ben E. King steps up to the mike, Ertegun tells King the story of the fat cripple watching another man dancing with his pretty new wife. King's eyes moisten, and he fights tears as he gives one of the most moving performances of his life.

Every actor knows you engage an audience more by fighting tears than by weeping.

Another example of the tipping point in art are the *ritratti parlanti* or "speaking likenesses" of Gian Lorenzo Bernini, his busts of people who, as Bernini himself said, seem either about to speak or to have just finished speaking. Look at the portraits the next time you walk through a gallery: the ones who say the most to you will be the ones who look as though they are about to come off the wall and tell you something, something you don't know yet, a thing that will change your life.

Emerson was fond of what he called *croisements* or "crossings," examples of which he gives in his *Journal*: "the seashore and the taste of two metals in contact, and our enlarged powers in the presence . . . of a friend." In his poem "Seashore," the sea addresses the reader, finishing this way: "Planting strange fruits and sunshine on the shore, / I make some coast alluring, some lone isle, / To distant men, who must go there, or die."

The traditional song "The House of the Rising Sun" ends with the singer saying he has "One foot on the platform / The other on the train."

What's the best part of roulette? When the wheel is spinning, and the ball hasn't found its slot yet. Of sex? Not orgasm but the moment just before, when you feel as though your whole body is about to explode. James Dickey said when you're masturbating, there's that feeling just before you come—that's poetry.

Everyone has a fascination with the world to come. If you make that world too distinct, who's going to want to go there? Robert Louis Stevenson said "to travel hopefully is a better thing than to arrive, and the true success is to labor." Taoists say "the journey is the reward."

I have a triptych on my study wall that used to be a quadtych; it shows the Eiffel Tower's construction stages in April, July, and December, 1888, but I cut off the last photo, the one showing the finished tower in May, 1889—as I read and write, I want to think about working, progressing, advancing, not completing.

What is it like to die? Most often, our last moments will be clouded by pain or drugs or fear, but it doesn't have to be that way. The poet Billy Collins told me that he was watching his mother die, and when he saw a change in her state, he asked her Caribbean sitter what she was doing, and the caretaker replied quietly, "She's traveling."

According to Claire Tomalin, his biographer, Thomas Hardy and his increasingly distant wife Emma, both fifty-nine, found common ground in their passion for bicycling, sometimes doing forty miles a day because "the English roads were rough and dusty, but they were also empty, the stagecoach having long disappeared and the motor-car not yet arrived, and so they had the best bicycling ever enjoyed."

Duke Ellington says, "My attitude is never to be satisfied, never enough, never."

The best time of the day is the moment after the last pushup and before the first martini.

You Aim Here to Strike over There

Recently I heard a marquee-name poet read slack, predictable poems to an adoring audience. As is often the case after a poetry reading these days, I came away not only disappointed but puzzled, though when I expressed my confusion, Barbara said, "That's what most people think poetry is."

At least the poet read about bucolic clichés: the bird he saw, the farmer who waved to him as he drove down a country road. Other poets who have left me flat recently write about themselves as well, but usually it's their horrible sex lives.

Or their wonderful sex lives: a year before, I'd heard a smiling middle-aged woman read a poem in which she tells her children that her husband, their father, "licked my asshole," a revelation intended to show that older folks have fun, too, though it only reminded me, not that some things should be kept private, but that there's an effective way to say virtually anything you want as well as a way that dramatizes the speaker's clumsiness.

There are a lot of ways to convey desire, but you don't do it by writing about anatomy.

When the marquee-name poet finished, an audience member asked him if it was painful for him to read deeply emotional poems in public, and he said no, that he only felt the emotions in his poems when he wrote them, and when he read them, they were just texts. Contrast this poet's deadness to his own words with the accounts of Charles Dickens' passionate public readings of the murder of Nancy in *Oliver Twist*, for example, or Allen Ginsberg's or James Dickey's recitations of their poems.

What doesn't work in writing is the rote, the familiar. In *Gravity and Grace*, Simone Weil writes of the "monotony of evil: never anything new, everything about it is *equivalent*. . . . That is hell itself." And indeed it is hell to sit in a hard chair for an hour and listen to something that you already know: birds are nice, farmers are nice, sex is sexy.

What a writer or any other artist should do—what a human being should do, be he or she Beethoven or a rec-room pianist, Julia Child or a guy making a sandwich for his kid—is add to the world and, in so doing, make a new world. The photographer Robert Doisneau, who chronicled life in Paris for a period of sixty years and whose best-known photo, "Kiss by the Hotel de Ville," has hung on thousands of dorm-room walls (and now web sites), said, "The world I tried to show was a world I would feel good in, where people would be kind, where I would find the affection that I wanted for myself. My photos were a sort of proof that such a world could exist."

This doesn't mean that an artist or anyone else always has to make a pleasant world; if art were only pleasant, we'd have very little of Virginia Woolf, no Poe or Kafka, less than half of Shakespeare, and only a few hundred of Emily Dickinson's more than 1700 poems. A made world can be one of terror or anticipation or revulsion; it can be a world that defies description. But the world an artist offers us must be *new*.

After all, isn't this what every artist wants to do, to convince us that his or her vision is what the world is, not what we see when we look to the left and right of us? Regardless of intent, every great artist convinces us that his or her world is the real one. A Michelangelo statue of a prisoner in the Accademia, say, or of Dawn waking atop a Medici tomb convinces you that people are really like that.

And then you look at the ones around you: the greasy-haired kid in the FUBAR t-shirt, the bearded guy whacking on his gum as though he's getting paid for every spitty crackle, even the big-hipped Spanish woman in tight jeans you imagine yawning and coming to wakefulness, her breasts spilling to the side as she raises her hand against the day's first light. And you think, No, people aren't that beautiful at all, or that well-proportioned, that tragic in the way they push against the flesh they're trapped in. And for a moment you're angry at the old guy talking loudly to his wife, the woman so big she can barely stand, yourself. And then you realize that this impossibility is at the heart of art's success, that art wouldn't work if real people were like statues.

Poets are "liberating gods" says Emerson in "The Poet," and he uses the phrase twice. "They are free, and they make free. An imaginative book renders much more service at first, by stimulating us through its tropes, than afterward when we arrive at the precise sense of the author."

Yes: precision is overrated. Stimulation is enough in itself.

How does the artist stimulate, though? In a May 6, 2009 piece in the *New York Times*, working-class Palestinian poet Taha Muhammed Ali says that writing poems is like playing billiards: you aim over here to strike over there. (Ali also says "The more mosques, the less poetry," but that's another essay.)

In *Watermark*, Brodsky says he doesn't like Pound's *Cantos* because "the main error was an old one: questing for beauty. For someone with such a long record of residence in Italy, it was odd that he hadn't realized that beauty can't be targeted, that it is always a by-product of other, often very ordinary pursuits."

Stax Records, home of Otis Redding and Wilson Pickett, reorganized in 1965 and quickly failed, which is when musician and producer Jim Dickinson said, "If they could have just gone back to using basically broken equipment and rednecks and stupid people, they would have stood a better chance."

I'll close out this part of my examination of indistinctness in poetry (sculpture, billiards, soul music) with two more quotes from musicians. While I'm talking to composer Carlisle Floyd about the Benjamin Britten opera *Peter Grimes*, Floyd tells me that Britten's storm music does the best job of any in evoking a storm without relying on musical illustration. I think I know what he means, but when I ask him what musical illustration is, Floyd says, "Music that sounds like a storm!"

According to Duke Ellington, "You've got to find some way of saying it without saying it."

A Bit Like a Magic Trick

When people ask me who my favorite American poet is, I say, "Shakespeare." For one thing, he not only predicted America with *The Tempest*, his great meditation on the beauties and cruelties of the New World, but also represented the collective yearning of the Old World as it all but leaned across the ocean to see what was on the other side.

What Shakespeare did for American poets specifically was to take advantage, like no one else, of English's double-sourced richness, its mix of sinuous Latinate polysyllables and brusque Anglo-Saxon grunts. Where would Melville, Whitman, Dickinson, Plath, Ginsberg and their fellow toilers on the slopes of Parnassus be without Shakespeare?

Shakespeare will always be our greatest writer, and an article from the December 19, 2006 issue of the *Toronto Star* explains why. "Researchers at the University of Liverpool have found one of Shakespeare's favorite linguistic tricks—throwing odd words into otherwise normal sentences or using a noun as an unexpected verb—surprises the brain in a way that generates a sudden burst of mental activity that actually shows up on a brain scan."

According to researcher Philip Davis of the University of Liverpool,

> When one word changes the grammar of a whole sentence, brain readings suddenly peak. The brain is then forced to re-trace its thinking process in order to understand what it is supposed to make of this unusual word. . . . By throwing odd words into seemingly normal sentences, Shakespeare actually surprises the brain in a manner that produces a sudden burst of activity—a sense of drama created out of the simplest things.

"The effect on the brain is a bit like a magic trick; we know what the trick means but we don't know how it happens—and instead of being confused in a negative sense, the brain is positively excited," says Neil Roberts, Davis's colleague.

The authors attached electrodes to the scalps of twenty people and read selected lines from Shakespeare's plays to measure brain response. As an example, Davis cites the phrase "he godded me" from *Coriolanus*, which is an unusual way of saying "he treated me like a god" that Davis says catches the brain off-guard. "It's like putting a jigsaw puzzle together; when you know how pieces fit, you can get bored, but if the pieces don't appear to fit at first, the brain becomes excited."

As poets, it's our job to write poems that get readers excited.

The early chapters of Peter Ames Carlin's biography of Brian Wilson deal with the Wilson brothers' complex relationship with their father, Murry, a notorious bully, yet a figure without whom the career of the Beach Boys would have been radically different or perhaps even non-existent. "Kick ass!" was Murry's mantra as he browbeat the boys through take after take, finding fault with everything and praising nothing as the sensitive Brian simultaneously withered under the treatment yet somehow sublimated it in a way that set the stage for the perfectionism that made him one of the authentic musical originals of the late twentieth century.

As poets, it's our job to kick ass.

As they learned their craft, the Beatles played a lengthy stint at a Hamburg club called the Indra which was managed by Bruno Koschmider, described by Beatles' biographer Bob Spitz as "a florid-faced man with a preposterous wig-like mop of hair." Koschmider would yell "*Mach schau!*" ("Put on a show!") during the boys' lackluster performances, and at first the four musicians laughed and staggered around, knocking over mikes as they made fun of the silly German man. But when the audiences went crazy, the boys saw the value of "putting on a show" and became the band that changed the world.

Not every poem "puts on a show," of course. But every great poem combines words in a quick and unexpected way that excites the brain. Take the phrase "wilderness of monkeys" that I use as my title. The phrase occurs in Act III of *The Merchant of Venice*, when Shylock learns that his faithless daughter traded a ring her dead mother gave him for a monkey and says, "I would not have given it for a wilderness of monkeys." Instantly we see the forest and the beasts, and we hear the howling—of the monkeys, of a father's broken heart, of our own.

Shakespeare makes it look easy. In the eighteenth century, Georg Christoph Lichtenberg wrote in a notebook that in the plays of Shakespeare "you often find remarks doing a kitchen-hand's work in some remote corner of a sentence which would deserve pride of place in a disquisition by any other writer."

When Macbeth kills Duncan, he frames the dead man's servants by wiping his hands on their sleeping faces and telling everyone that he found them "badged with blood." Shakespeare doesn't make a big deal out of this; he just drops in "badged" where the rest of us would have said "smeared" or "splashed." And the effect is that much greater. As with "a wilderness of monkeys," our brains are surprised "in a manner that produces a sudden burst of activity," as the two University of Liverpool researchers say, and the effect is indelible.

As Duke Ellington said about jazz, "It's like an act of murder; you play with intent to commit something."

What, though? You're not quite sure. We're often disappointed in the way a poem or story or movie ends because the ending is either too decisive or not decisive enough. Or maybe the whole thing is too obvious. "We hate poetry that has a palpable design upon us," says Keats.

But a phrase, some verbal sleight of hand, a gesture that's indistinct, one that promises something beyond itself—that's what we want. We want a soundless day, low clouds, and a man on horseback passing through a dreary land, his heart brimming with desire.

Works Cited

Note: The books mentioned in this essay are cited below. In the interest of space, sources for song references and short quotes from poems, stories and other works in the public domain are not given; readers will find these on the internet, as I did. In the interest of consistency, I end each of my four sections with a quotation from Duke Ellington, though it should be noted that Ellington takes "A man is a god in ruins" from Emerson's essay "Nature."

Brodsky, Joseph. *Watermark*. New York: Farrar, 1993. Print.

Carlin, Peter Ames. *Catch a Wave: The Rise, Fall, and Redemption of the Beach Boys' Brian Wilson*. Emmaus, PA: Rodale, 2007. Print.

Carey, John. *What Good Are the Arts?* New York: Oxford UP, 2006. Print.

Davis, Philip. "Reading Shakespeare Has Dramatic Effect on Human Brain." *Toronto Star*, 19 December 2006. Print.

Fisher, Marc. *Something in the Air: Radio, Rock, and the Revolution That Shaped a Generation*. New York: Random House, 2007. Print.

Garner, Dwight. "A Merchant of Trinkets and Memories." Rev. of *My Happiness Bears No Relation to Happiness: A Poet's Life in the Palestinian Century*, Adina Hoffman. *New York Times*, 5 May 2009. Print.

Greenblatt, Stephen. *Will in the World: How Shakespeare Became Shakespeare*. New York: Norton, 2004. Print.

Halberstadt, Alex. *Lonely Avenue: The Unlikely Life and Times of Doc Pomus*. New York: Da Capo, 2007. Print.

Iser, Wolfgang. *The Act of Reading: A Theory of Aesthetic Response*. Baltimore: Johns Hopkins UP, 1978. Print.

Marcus, Greil. *Lipstick Traces: A Secret History of the Twentieth Century*. London: Martin, 1989. Print.

Marlow, Ann. *How to Stop Time: Heroin from A to Z*. New York: Anchor, 2000. Print.

Mouton, Todd. "Backtalk with Cosimo Matassa." *Offbeat*, 1 November 2007. Print.

Spitz, Bob. *The Beatles: The Biography*. New York: Little, 2005. Print.

Tomalin, Claire. *Thomas Hardy*. London: Penguin, 2007. Print.

Weil, Simone. *Gravity and Grace*. New York: Putnam, 1952. Print.

Willis, Ellen. *Beginning to See the Light: Sex, Hope, and Rock-and-Roll*. Middletown: Wesleyan UP, 1992. Print.

Hybrid Aesthetics and Its Discontents

Arielle Greenberg, Craig Santos Perez,
Michael Theune, Megan Volpert, and Mark Wallace

I n his introduction to his anthology *American Poetry Since 1950*, Eliot
Weinberger states that "[f]or decades, American poetry has been
divided into two camps" (qtd. in Swensen xvii). This division has
been described in a variety of ways, many of which are touched upon in
Cole Swensen's introduction to *American Hybrid: A Norton Anthology of New
Poetry* (the publication of which provided the occasion for the following
papers), including Robert Lowell's "the cooked and the uncooked," Paul
Auster's tracking of British and French poetic legacies in American
poetry, and Swensen's own notion that the divide separates two different
"concepts of meaning": the "transcendent" and the "immanent" (xvii-
xviii). This divide has manifested itself in the American poetry wars,
which pitted Language poets against Official Verse Culture. And more
recently, this divide has been described by poet and critic Ron Silliman
as a divide between Post-Avant poetry and the School of Quietude.
Regardless of the particular terminology, this divide typically has been
described as one between avant-garde experimentalism and more traditional, or at least mainstream, lyric practice.

At present, numerous editors, anthologists, and critics are trying to
move beyond such distinctions. Recognizing the effort on the part of
many poets to forge a style that draws from both sides of the divide,

these editors work to reveal the emerging synthesis of the experimental and the lyrical in spaces Reginald Shepherd (himself a central hybrid anthologist and theorist) defines as "the intersections between lyric enchantment and experimental interrogation" (*Lyric* xi). The work that grows out of such efforts goes by many names, including "Third Way," "Elliptical," and, most recently, now, "Hybrid."

Growing interest in the hybrid (the term we'll use here) constitutes a significant trend in contemporary American poetry. The idea has been percolating for approximately the past two decades: in Alice Fulton's writing on fractal poetics; in Stephen Burt's writing on the Ellipticism, including "The Elliptical Poets" and "Close Calls with Nonsense"; in "Principles for Formal Experimentation," the final section of Annie Finch and Katherine Varnes's *An Exaltation of Forms*; and in David Caplan's *Questions of Possibility: Contemporary Poetry and Poetic Form*. And it has flourished more recently in the publication of a handful of anthologies, including Claudia Rankine and Juliana Spahr's *American Women Poets in the 21st Century: Where Lyric Meets Language*, and *The Iowa Anthology of New American Poetries* and *Lyric Postmodernisms: An Anthology of Contemporary Innovative Poetries*, both edited by Reginald Shepherd. Additionally, as evidenced by the roster of poets involved with key hybrid publications—among them: Jorie Graham, C. D. Wright, Donald Revell, and Bin Ramke—the hybrid is an aesthetic featured at some of America's top-tier creative writing programs; in fact, it might be deemed the central aesthetic of both the Iowa and Brown MFA programs.

Hybrid poetry most recently has been defined and promoted by the publication of *American Hybrid*, edited by Cole Swensen and David St. John. Besides being the newest, *American Hybrid* is also the most significant collection of hybrid work to date. Including seventy-four poets, it certainly is the biggest. It also is the most well-known; it has garnered a great deal of attention. At the 2009 conference of the Association of Writers and Writing Programs, *American Hybrid* was featured and championed in a reading and a panel presentation. It also has attracted some critical commentary, especially in the blogosphere. In "Nonsense/Burt/Hybrid," a post on his *Exoskeleton* blog, Johannes Göransson finds that the hybrid tends toward the aesthetically conservative; he states, "Behind the overt quietism vs langpo model for the hybrid, I think there's a more fundamental idea of the poetics of moderation, of hybrids between crassness and pure formalism" (par. 16). At *Silliman's Blog*, Ron Silliman critiques the failed synthesis of hybridity, stating, "Hybridism wants to be new & it wants to be the well-wrought urn. For the most part, it accomplishes neither. Above all else, it is a failure of courage" (par. 5).

The following five papers continue this critical conversation, considering if and how the hybrid has changed the aesthetic, cultural, and ideological implications of the mainstream/avant-garde distinction, looking at the extent to which supposedly boundary-crossing hybrid aesthetics have or have not been truly transformative, examining and appraising it to determine its potential and its problems. In "Against Unity," Mark Wallace challenges the application of what he sees as the overly simple two-camp model to a much more complex contemporary American poetry scene, and, while he continues to call for hybridity in poetry, the hybridity he hopes for is a stranger, even more monstrous kind of hybridity than is found in *American Hybrid*. In "No Laughing Matter: The Humorless Hybrid," Michael Theune reveals that hybridity, while meant to synthesize, in fact reinscribes a significant division in American poetry: that between the serious and the comedic. In "Hybridity in Gurlesque Poetry," Arielle Greenberg considers another kind of hybridity, the Gurlesque, a more extreme and vigorous hybrid than is typically encountered in hybrid anthologies. Both Craig Santos Perez and Megan Volpert reveal the culturally conservative trends in hybrid anthologizing; in "Whitewashing American Hybrid Aesthetics," Perez critiques *American Hybrid* for not representing America's racial and ethnic diversity, and in "A Drag Queen's Lament: Or, how I learned to stop worrying and love my camp," Volpert critiques the relatively conservative sexual politics of hybridity and calls for a poetry of unapologetic, queer difference.

These papers, sometimes in edited versions, were presented in the "Hybrid Aesthetics and Its Discontents" panel, organized by Michael Theune and Mark Wallace, at the 2010 Association of Writers and Writing Programs Conference in Denver, Colorado. Thus, though they in fact interact in some significant and even fascinating ways, sharing critiques and perspectives, and though they were composed in response to an identical "panel description" required by the AWP, these papers were not composed with a full knowledge each of the other's undertakings and findings, and so there is occasional slippage and overlap. One basic fact that all the papers seem to agree upon is that there is no problem with hybridity *per se* (indeed many of the following papers champion hybridity), just with how it so far has been theorized and anthologized. A significant difference among the papers is the particular target of their critique: in Perez's and Volpert's papers, the critique is aimed directly at *American Hybrid*; Theune's paper also focuses on *American Hybrid*, but takes aim at hybrid anthologizing practices, and the results of those practices, more broadly; in Wallace's and Greenberg's papers, the critique (largely implicit in Greenberg's essay) is aimed at the somewhat limiting ways that hybridity, in its various names, has been framed, theorized, and defined. However, regardless of these slight though significant differences, all of the papers presented here work together to critically and intelligently extend the conversation of and about, and to engage a new, vital but also problematic development within, contemporary American poetry.

Against Unity
Mark Wallace

> And the followers of Namirrha were the dead of strange kingdoms, the demons of sky and earth and the abyss, and the mad, impious, hybrid things that the sorcerer himself created from forbidden unions.
> —CLARK ASHTON SMITH, "THE DARK EIDOLON"

In one of his overwrought, Modernist art deco (and morally conventional) horror fantasies, "The Dark Eidolon," Clark Ashton Smith, a compatriot of H. P. Lovecraft, describes a notion of the hybrid helpful for thinking about contemporary poetics. Smith's definition provides a worthwhile vantage point for considering the shortcomings of hybrid literature as it has been defined in the *American Hybrid* anthology as well as in a related series of anthologies and terminologies, including *Lyric Postmodernisms*, *The Iowa Anthology of New Poetries*, and the notion of "third way poetics."

Hybrid things, in Smith's formulation, are the opposite of pious ones. The deformed births of creatures who never should have mated, these hybrids were not supposed to exist, although the issue of who supposes so is crucial. The host of hybrids that should not exist, but do, are linked not simply to what has existed and been forgotten but also to what has been rightly forgotten by all right-thinking people.

Smith was primarily a playfully grim aesthete. Anyone who knows anything about Lovecraft, however, who was perhaps the most important writer to publish in *Weird Tales* in the 20s and 30s, knows that for Lovecraft the essential impure hybrid was racial miscegenation. Yet Lovecraft's virulent racism masks an even deeper fear of any sexual contact whatsoever. In Lovecraft's fiction, almost all sexual unions seem forbidden. It's not so much that some creatures shouldn't touch but that touching itself is disgusting.

A literary version of Smith's hybrid would reject the belief that something is best when untouched (that is, uncorrupted) by things outside it. The value of the untouched thing remains an assumed good in many contemporary discourses, including political, cultural, and literary ones. Use of the word "object" for instance is usually marked by singularity: an object holds together, is distinct. Artistic objects have often been discussed in terms of their structural or thematic unity. The same is true for concepts of tradition, school, or movement: if those are distinguished by similarity rather than untouched purity, they are still marked by a unity that defines itself through what it rejects. A tradition whose values have changed beyond recognition is no longer a tradition. A school that has no unity, whether of theme or technique, is simply not a school. Denying that your particular group of similarly-inclined artists has anything in common is the same as denying that they even are a group.

In literature, the hybrid distorts the normal unifying marks of many literary concepts. Genre, technique, tradition, or the identifying marks of a movement or school: in the hybrid, all these things are subject to mismatching and deforming. Yet in many recent poetry anthologies, a seeming belief in the hybrid's impure multiplicity ends up being used as a way of reinforcing a pure singularity. Belief in unity seems to hang on tenaciously even when invoking a hybridity that seems meant to displace it. Like too many readings of Lovecraft, we can be too quick to celebrate that we are not racists while remaining unaware of how many ways we continue to live with the fear of being touched.

Perhaps no concept better represents confusion between desire for the multiple and for the pure singular as the political notion of The People. Is it singular or plural? Of course the word means more than one person. Add a definite article though and the phrase, "The People," is also singular, one of those tricky group entity singular nouns. When "The people speak with one voice," as during the French Revolution, when the concept of The People was a highly efficient tool for killing people, are they many or are they one?

The literary question is, how has the tension between the singular and the plural, the pure and impure, people and The People, the solid object and the melted one, the traditional and anti-traditional, the (singular and multiple) school or group and the (also singular and sometimes multiple) individual writer manifested itself in recent poetics discussions about the value of hybridity? And how much of the problem depends on the definition of hybridity that one works with?

I first began thinking in the early 90s about the disruptive, impure, and nightmarish possibilities of hybrid aesthetics. It has influenced a great deal of my writing and played a hidden but essential role in the essays gathered in the anthology I edited with Steven Marks, *Telling It Slant: Avant Garde Poetics of the 1990s*, a text that has not been mentioned often in recent discussions of hybrid aesthetics.

To my thinking during the 90s, hybridity challenged ideas of singularity and purity that I saw as much among writers invested in avant garde, experimental, or non-traditional approaches to literature (feel free to pick your own singular term and its own singular problems) as among writers who denied that those alternatives had value or that they themselves were part of a tradition (if there are no alternatives, a tradition isn't a tradition, it's simply "all there is"). I noted then something that remains true today: the need to define poetry by the singular, and the fear of the inchoate chaos that might result if one does not, remains a guiding principle of many poetics discussions.

The fear is related to fears about loss of identity, loss of a public profile, and finally loss of all attention. It is related to the fear of democracy both in politics and in poetry, or at least to the fear that democracy might actually be the same as chaos (or its more passive version, an "everything goes" liberalism). I don't intend simply to criticize such fears, to suggest that the world of poetry will be healed (is it sick, and if it was, mightn't one want that?) by getting over them. There are worthwhile concerns nestled within the often troubling ways these fears manifest themselves, a point I'll return to.

My own essay in *Telling It Slant*, "Towards a Free Multiplicity of Form," focused on the relation between literary technique, historical context, and social group dynamics among poets. I suggested that it was increasingly unlikely that poets would know only, or work only within, one literary tradition. Instead, many poets now work with an awareness of multiple and global poetic traditions. Insistence on the primacy of any single literary tradition seems more than ever like narrow-minded provincialism. I also raised questions about the relation between innovative literary technique and political/cultural radicalism; historically, those two don't always match, although manifestos about radical literary techniques frequently align themselves with the desire for large scale social revolution. At the time of the essay's writing in the mid-90s, there were at least five different, broadly successful schools of thought in U.S. poetry: traditional formalist poetry; MFA narrative and lyrical free verse poetry; a more overtly political poetry of identity raising issues of culture, race, gender, and class; New American poetry; and the New American offshoot of Language poetry and other radical aesthetic, often politicized approaches.

At the time, describing U.S. poetry production that way was already overly schematic (something I acknowledged) even as the world of poetry was further changing and splintering. But if there was in the mid-90s a minimum of five major schools of poetic thought in the U.S., the idea of a two party-system (for instance, Ron Silliman's split between School of Quietude and New American poetries, which has more significance historically than currently), or the notion of a "third way" (which was, at best, in the late 90s no more than a sixth way) was even then an oversimplification. And if trying to isolate U.S. poetic production from the larger global contexts with which it interacts is closer to troubling nationalism than accurate description, the idea of there being only two or three approaches quickly becomes ludicrous.

Not unexpectedly, while the published reviews of *Telling It Slant* were on the whole positive, the work in that anthology, and of the writers associated with it, was sometimes criticized for lacking direction, or some similar problem that comes down simply to lacking an obvious singularity of poetics. It was conveniently overlooked that the introduction that Steven and I wrote highlighted that the anthology purposefully intended to refuse singular answers while pointing to shared questions and the essential importance of disagreement, or that many of the essays were critical of traditions that defined themselves as singular or pure. The anthology did not highlight a singular poetics and therefore, for some people, did not create a recognizable identity. Did not do, that is, what an anthology of contemporary writing is supposed to do.

Telling It Slant did not appear in a vacuum, of course. Many writers shared some of my ideas about the values of disunity (see for instance Steve Evans' introduction to the *Writing from the New Coast* anthology, although I disagreed with Evans' assertion that the writing which similarly interested us was in any shared sense anti-identity). Many others felt that what was needed were new movements, new schools that could be identified as such. Attempts to forge new group identities emerged in the 90s around the magazine *Apex of the M*, with its editorial insistence that American experimental poetries had neglected spirituality, or in the now long forgotten New Synthesis proposed by John Noto and others. There were also pseudo-groups created to make fun of the group identity impulse; for example, the Bay area's New Brutalism, which came several years later, seems primarily to have been a joke. Nowhere is the group impulse and anti-group impulse more connected than in the currently both popular and reviled Flarf group, in which a group in-joke about writing bad poetry turned into a real school of poetics with a now widely recognized name. Flarf is definitely a group but it also makes fun of the group tendency through such practices as K. Silem Mohammad's ironic, consciously collapsing manifestos.

In circles which had closer connection than I did to the production mechanisms of the 1990s MFA industry, similar responses to poetry group formation were at work. One manifested itself in the anthologies *Lyric Postmodernisms* and *The Iowa Anthology of New Poetries* edited by the late Reginald Shepherd and another, after lurking for years, emerged more clearly in the 2009 anthology *American Hybrid* edited by Cole Swensen and David St. John. In these anthologies, a different notion of hybrid emerged. This notion of hybrid tries to find similarity across divergent practices. It breaks down the idea of singular schools by looking for things different poetic groups have in common. It tries to find middle ground. It imagines itself, perhaps, as a new center, one from which the most extreme and divisive elements of divergent practices have been tempered or simply removed. In this imagining, it asserts a power relationship between and over various practices, one in which this new center masters the flaws and excesses of divergent schools of thought, in theory taking the best of each and disregarding the rest.

In rejecting excess and extremes, this notion of hybrid recalls Hegel's concept of synthesis, which at least the no longer discussed approach of John Noto was willing to name directly. For Hegel, a prior set of competing claims in any given discourse is resolved by a synthesis of those claims, one which forms a new central idea. Of course that synthesis, when successful, is according to Hegel soon opposed again, an issue that most attempts at synthesizing contemporary poetry fail to recognize.

The notion of hybrid as synthesis seeks to undermine older competing unities but does so in the name of creating a new, inclusive (but also exclusive) non-competing unity. It's fascinating that a concept of hybridity, of disrupting the singular, should become a way of creating a new singular. As if one might use a new concept of transgression in order to tame old transgressions. As if the notion of hybridity can become a normative new that can keep monstrous hybrids from being born.

In various essays and reviews, Michael Theune has been tracing the problems in Shepherd's and related notions of third way poetics. As just one example, Theune notes that some of the selections in Shepherd's anthologies reflect personal aesthetic preferences that have little to do with the dividing line between mainstream and experimental practices. Classical references, and their predominance among the poems Shepherd chooses, seem to have little to do with the issues at stake, unless we imagine that a love of classical gardens is the thing that, before now, most U.S. poets were afraid to recognize that they all shared. And as Johannes Göransson pointed out in his review of *American Hybrid*, to make the case that the anthology is creating a middle ground between two long-warring camps, the editors "caricature a multiplicity of styles as two extremes" (par. 4). A more successful anthology is *American Women Poets in the 21st Century: Where Lyric Meets Language*, edited by Claudia Rankine and Juliana Spahr, which selects work by and about a small group of women writers whose approaches might seem at first glance opposed to each other. But that anthology makes no claim to find similarity across the total ground of contemporary U.S. poetry, although Spahr's introduction addresses problems with seeing "lyric" and "language" as synonyms for two warring groups.

I think it's safe to say therefore that anthologies attempting to establish middle ground between various U.S. poetry practices have not done so. And they certainly could not do so by attempting to create a new middle in American poetry based on combining or overcoming the limitations of what is supposedly only two prior camps.

There have now been about fifteen years of claims that the distinction between so-called "mainstream" and "avant garde" literatures are increasingly irrelevant. And in fact the contemporary poetic landscape shows that to be true. But that's not because poetry exists in any greater state of unity than before. Just the opposite: probably we have more differing claims than ever regarding the value of contemporary poetry. *American Hybrid* and Shepherd's anthologies represent not a new middle ground but instead posit specific schools of thought that oppose themselves to other schools of thought.

In fact, schools of thought may now appear and disappear more rapidly than ever. The appearance of anthologies supporting the apparent growth of the concepts of third way poetics and *American Hybrid* may in fact signal that those concepts have already peaked and may quickly become relics (perhaps even abandoned relics) of a now gone era. I also wonder whether new approaches can genuinely be created by editors. I think terminologies have more staying power when writers self-identify as a group. Nada Gordon, for instance, considers herself an ongoing member of the Flarf group, yet I doubt that Rae Armantrout considers herself a poet of a Hybrid School. Quite literally, there is no such school, although I doubt that Armantrout would consider herself a member of it if it did exist.

U.S. poetry in almost all recent anthologies and in much poetry criticism and discussion still seems based on differing, often competing groups, with various terminologies defining publications, blogs, and websites, although most groups highlight the multiplicity of approaches that can be harbored safely within them. There are now Flarf and Gurlesque anthologies. The development of the Plumbline School, a poetics of moderation and balance recently named by Henry Gould and compatriots will, despite Gould's constant mockery of the notion of schools, be ultimately measured by the writing that does or does not appear in relationship to the name of the group. There is no such thing as an anti-group poetics that brings together all (or even a significant portion) of the varying groups that exist. Attempts to do so usually just create further groups.

Certainly we have no anthology of contemporary poetry that successfully critiques the notion of the singular school or highlights the range of differences and disagreements that currently exists. A recent issue of *Poetry Magazine* that featured Flarf and conceptual writing in one section and more conventional narrative and lyric verse in another was an intriguing, if overly cautious, example of at least a small-scale attempt. Approaches that come closest can still be found more within anthologies that consciously embrace experimental extremes rather than those that attempt to tame them.

For instance, *Wreckage of Reason: An Anthology of Contemporary Xxperimental Prose by Women Writers,* edited by Nava Renek, features more distinctively and outrageously hybrid texts than any recent poetry anthology. It includes works that variously mix poetry, prose, fiction, memoir, criticism, taboo language, self-reflexive commentary, instructional manuals, visual art, processual text (computer-generated and not), as well as much else. Many of the hybrid texts in that anthology are not designed to smooth over differences between ways of writing, but instead show how differences collide with and question each other.

But even if there were poetry anthologies that highlighted, rather than attempting to minimize or avoid, differences across groups, those anthologies would create not a new center but just another way of think-ing. Although U.S. poets continue to have difficulty accepting difference or even acknowledging its value, and factionalism creates hostility and furthers existing resource imbalances, I don't think that trying to end factionalism is a suitable response to the existence of so many approach-es. Factionalism isn't going to end. Any new claim to end it will only be opposed by further factionalism.

And in many ways that's how it should be. The huge energy of fac-tionalism, of aesthetic and cultural disagreement, shows just how many and different are the people who remain committed to the value of poetry, especially in a country (and perhaps a world) where we're often told that no one values it at all. Part of that factionalism involves the fear of being unknown or forgotten (right now as well as forever) and the anti-dem-ocratic fear that too many points of view equals a chaotic loss of defined value. But it also exists because poets, defying supposed good sense, continue to believe that their poetry and their ideas about it matter.

I hope that my conviction that we should resist trying to make the multiple into a singular will not be confused with lacking direction. My commitment remains to poetic innovation and extremes and to their connection to other forms of cultural awareness and action, both on local and global levels. There are histories to borrow from and remem-ber, but there are no models sufficient to guide the present or future of poems. Poems that attempt simply to reflect poetry's past, or to see in it a bedrock source of value, will never be sufficient to deal with the always-changing present. It's difficult to feel optimistic about global political conditions and the role of the U.S. in them. Even if one is optimistic, that can only be on the grounds of the continued possibility of change.

What we need are poems that understand and challenge the present while being aware that the present itself is both a function of the past and an inevitable rewriting of it, for better or worse, since history hardly involves pure progress. We need poems that take aesthetic risks and explore new techniques and provide new cultural insights. Still, I doubt that poems of that kind are going to arise solely within the work of one poetic school or from one or two poets of greatness. We need to recog-nize that profoundly different approaches to contemporary poetry lead to many varieties of worthwhile poems. Yet we should acknowledge that there's no overarching framework that can bring all those approaches together without conflict.

No Laughing Matter: The Humorless Hybrid
Michael Theune

In her introduction to *American Hybrid*, Cole Swensen defines and describes the hybrid poem, stating,

> Today's hybrid poem might engage such conventional approaches as narrative that presumes a stable first person, yet complicate it by disrupting the linear temporal path or by scrambling the normal syntactical sequence. Or it might foreground recognizably experimental modes such as illogicality or fragmentation, yet follow the strict formal rules of a sonnet or a villanelle. Or it might be composed entirely of neologisms but based in ancient traditions. Considering the traits associated with "conventional" work, such as coherence, linearity, formal clarity, narrative, firm closure, symbolic resonance, and stable voice, and those generally assumed of "experimental" works, such as nonlinearity, juxtaposition, rupture, fragmentation, immanence, multiple perspective, open form, and resistance to closure, hybrid poets access a wealth of tools, each one of which can change dramatically depending on how it is combined with others and the particular role it plays in the composition. (xxi)

For Swensen, the value of such poetry is its ability to synthesize. Hybrid poetry is poetry that situates itself in the middle space formed by what is often conceived of as what Swensen calls the "fundamental division" in twentieth-century American poetry (xvii). Formulated in a variety of ways (Romantic vs. Modern; New Formal vs. Language), this division typically comes down to a divide between more mainstream, traditional poetries and more avant-garde, radically experimental poetries, in Swensen's words, "the two-camp model" (xvii). According to Swensen, the poetry in *American Hybrid* is new insofar as it hybridizes "core attributes of previous 'camps' in diverse and unprecedented ways" (xvii). Swensen states, "The hybrid poem has selectively inherited traits from both of the principal paths . . ." (xxi).

The result, according to Swensen, is a "thriving center of alterity" (xx). (And my sense is that this is the view of the other main hybrid anthologist, Reginald Shepherd, who makes anthologies with plurals in the titles—*The Iowa Anthology of New American Poetries*, *Lyric Postmodernisms*—but anthologies that also are designed to collect poems that are hybrid, work that, according to the first sentence of the introduction to *Lyric Postmodernisms*, "combines lyricism and avant-garde experimentation in a new synthesis" (xi).) However, I think we need to be clear that this "thriving center of alterity" does in fact already have its outsider others. They are, on the one hand, the poets of plainspoken, accessible poetry: stand-up, ultra-talk, and slam poets. That is, just as Stephen Burt claims about Elliptical poetry in "What I Miss in What I Like," the final section of his essay "Close Calls with Nonsense" (the second of his two essays on Elliptical poetry), *American Hybrid* could be said to be "missing" poetry by those "devoted more straight-forwardly to argument and wit" (18). The missing poetry, on the other hand, is the poetry that is more carnivalesque—perhaps funny, but, if so, more clownish, odd, disturbing, shocking, abjectly surreal.

It shocks me how very unfunny—whether gently humorous or out-and-out slapstick—hybrid anthologies are. I want to think this fact through a bit because it is very strange: this very clear divide seems to duplicate just the problems the hybrid was supposed to resolve. However, instead of signaling the end of the two-camp model—or, as Reginald Shepherd puts it in his essay "One State of the Art," the "unnuanced either/or thinking," the "territorialization and fence-building" (4–5), he charged the avant-garde and the mainstream as having—hybrid thinking reinstates it, and it does so in the most traditional and predictable of ways: separating the (seeming) serious and the comic, the (supposed) high and the low.

What's especially odd, though, is that this most obvious feature of the hybrid is never discussed by the anthologists as a crucial feature of the hybrid. Did the hybrid anthologists do this unknowingly? It's possible. Swensen (and St. John) and Shepherd are not exactly poets of humor and wit. Their anthologies may largely be the result of being the effect of an editor's unthinking (or at least unannounced) personal tastes and predilections. However, I also want to suggest that it may be something else: that there is in the thinking about hybrid poetry a kind of cordoning off of the humorous. Take for example the fact that even the work of some of the great wits and comedians who are included in some of these anthologies—including D. A. Powell and Dean Young—is toned down, that some of their funniest and most extreme and wonderful poems are excluded. For example, nowhere is to be found D. A. Powell's excellent, lovely, hilarious poem, "dogs and boys can treat you like trash. And dogs do love trash," the opening stanzas of which read,

> dogs and boys can treat you like trash.　and dogs do love trash
> to nuzzle their muzzles.　they slather with tongues that smell like
>   their nuts
>
> but the boys are fickle when they lick you.　they stick you with twigs
> and roll you over like roaches.　then off with another: those sluts
>
> with their asses so tight you couldn't get them to budge for a turd
> so unlike the dogs: who will turn in a circle showing & showing their
>   butts (14)

I want to pursue such exclusions a bit. Even though many of the poets included in hybrid anthologies, such as Powell and Young, are really what I would call "mixed mode" poets, poets who may at times write a seemingly hybrid poem but who really work in a variety of modes, sometimes writing hybrid, sometimes writing something much more in line with, say, a plainspoken, mainstream (not to mention humorous, or even hilarious) poem, such real mixedness (a mixedness, I must emphasize, that runs not only though poetry but poets . . .) is reduced and homogenized: the stand out, and especially the humorous, poetry is largely omitted.

And I think there is a significant reason for this: the inclusion of such poetry would reveal a glaring limitation of the hybrid: it cannot create such effects. Humor requires great orchestration, the management of great, playful leaps. What the hybrid, with its recombinations, its disruptions and scramblings (which very often come to seem like, and which hybrid thinking so far has done nothing to differentiate from, mere *short-circuiting*) has real trouble creating is wit. Wit—recognized as one of the rarest of all poetic achievements; in his essay "Andrew Marvell," T. S. Eliot calls wit "something precious and needed . . ." (263)—is such a precious achievement because in order to create it one must create a sense of fitting surprise, a state in which language both delivers on expectations yet leaps beyond them. As Barbara Herrnstein Smith notes in *Poetic Closure: A Study of How Poems End*, "A hyperdetermined conclusion will have maximal stability and finality; and when these qualities occur in conjunction with unexpected or in some way unstable material . . . the result will be *wit*—which, as many have observed, occurs when expectations are simultaneously surprised and fulfilled" (206). *Wit* requires a *real* synthesis, and humor requires the skillful, effective combination of attentiveness to the brain and the guts and the groin. The hybrid offers no vision of what a *successful* recombination of poetic elements is; though it talks of synthesis, its poems don't have to have wit's synthesis, and rather are allowed to be messy amalgamations. Perhaps exquisite, singular poetic syntheses are omitted from hybrid anthologies because they would put to the test the value of hybridity in general.

Even if I'm wrong about the above speculations, it is clear that the hybrid, as it has been theorized and anthologized by Shepherd and Swensen (and St. John), is squeamish about the boldly, bodily bawdy. Indeed, the hybrid of Shepherd, Swensen, and St. John could be seen as a prudish poetry of titillation. Thankfully, another kind of poetics, another kind of hybridity, is on the rise: Arielle Greenberg's Gurlesque. Depending upon how carnivalesque it really is (and isn't the carnivalesque the location of the "thriving center of alterity"?), the Gurlesque has great potential to dethrone and disempower *American Hybrid,* just as the carnival's fool and boy (or gurl) did the king and bishop. I look forward to hearing and reading much more about this other kind of hybrid aesthetic.

Two decades ago, in "Can Poetry Matter?," an essay in which, we should recall, it is argued that "a clubby feeling . . . typifies most recent anthologies of contemporary poetry" (7) and that "[a]nthologies . . . should not be used as pork barrels for the creative writing trade" (20), Dana Gioia states, "It is time to experiment, time to leave the well-ordered but stuffy classroom, time to restore a vulgar vitality to poetry . . ." (21). Our poets have been experimenting, but the hybrid anthologists have not, offering little that is truly new, sticking to standard modes, and in the process reinscribing the same kinds of stuffy distinctions that their work was meant to overcome.

Hybridity in Gurlesque Poetry
Arielle Greenberg

In this essay, I'm going to be discussing the hybrid as I see it used in poetry which I call "Gurlesque," a term I coined to describe certain poems by younger American women poets. I'm co-editor of an anthology by this name, and there's more about the Gurlesque below. But first I want to be very clear that the definition of hybrid I'm *not* working with is the notion of the hybrid as hovering between several aesthetic strains, as in the poetry (like my own) which pulls together threads of confessional, lyric, experimental and whatever other styles are out there. I think of that work through Stephen Burt's term "Elliptical" or I think of the idea of poems that are on a "fence" between aesthetics, which is one way Rebecca Wolff has talked about the name of her press and magazine and the work that appears therein.

Instead, the definition I'm working with is the hybrid as uncategorizable as any particular strain of poetry, or even as a poem. Work that defies genre and medium. Work that shape-shifts as it goes along, that strains against convention (*any* convention! even avant-garde convention!), is undefinable or between definitions, between aesthetics. Work that is truly on the margins or in the ditches. I like how Mark Wallace (above) describes the work in the prose anthology of experimental women's writing *Wreckage of Reason* as texts that are not designed to smooth over ruptures between ways of writing, but instead to emphasize how differences collide with and question each other. This is exactly how I would describe the poetry I call Gurlesque, and exactly the kind of hybridity in which I am interested.

And I'm not "discontent" with the hybrid as thus defined. I don't want to say I'm *content*, exactly, because I think by its nature the hybrid seeks to destabilize and discomfort, but I am thrilled by such poetry, inspired by it, a champion of it. This doesn't mean I think it's aproblematic, but you won't be hearing a complaint against this kind of hybridity from me.

I actually have been telling my undergraduate and graduate students for years that this definition of hybrid-genre work is where it's at, is where we're headed in literature, is what's most exciting about what's being written right now. To my mind, this kind of hybrid work is the best match for our early twenty-first century moment, for our current understanding of time and communication, for the blurred borders that offer the most promise and best reflect our complex reality.

In the rationale for this panel, the hybrid is described as a "Third Way." I would venture that the hybrid poetics I'm about to describe, the Gurlesque, are not a Third Way but Third Wave, from a feminist lens.

Before I explain the ways in which I think it's hybrid, what is a Gurlesque poetics? I came up with the term in 2001 as a way to describe something I was seeing cropping up in the most compelling new poetry I was reading by American women poets of my own generation. The term, which is a conscious mash-up and nod to other literary theories and cultural phenomena including the grotesque, the carnivalesque, burlesque, and the riot grrl punk and zine movement, describes work which performs femininity in a campy or overtly mocking manner, risking being inappropriate, offensive, outlandish, even repulsive, shaking the foundations of acceptable female behavior and language as previously used in poetry. The poets I see employing these strategies seemed to feel the license to be sly, overblown, outrageous, funny, and obscene about topics that were previously held up as Serious in feminist American poetry and demanded to be treated seriously, things like rape and body image and consumer culture. These poets employed sequins and unicorns and all sort of ephemera hitherto considered downright embarrassing to put in a poem. (There are also visual artists making some wonderful examples of work of a parallel aesthetic in our Gurlesque anthology. And it's happening in music, too: I'd look to folks including Björk, Joanna Newsom, and CocoRosie. The Gurlesque in rock music is a topic I'd love to write about more sometime soon. And there is much more to say about the historic, literary, and cultural origins and lineage of the Gurlesque, but for that you'll have to buy the anthology and look elsewhere!)

In the Gurlesque, girliness is key, and the main way I think Gurlesque poetry is genuinely subversive is its desire to put the girly—imagery, vernacular, topics, and tone—in the forefront of the work, challenging those who encounter it to find it "ditsy" or "shallow" or "slutty" or "dumb." The radical irreverence the Gurlesque poets apply to such topics, and everything else they write about, including poetry itself, seems to me very much grounded in Third Wave strategies in the way it presents the feminine as playful, carnal, over-the-top, and highly politically-charged all at once.

I want to be clear that although I enjoy and feel challenged in some wonderful ways by poetry I deem to be Gurlesque, my intention is not to champion it over other kinds of poetry, or to make it a club, or any such thing. I actually don't consider my own poetics Gurlesque (which is something that I feel gets misunderstood when it's written about by others). I just think it's really exciting that women poets are utilizing some brazen and newish approaches to gender perfomativity in poetry these days. I don't think it's the only kind of feminist writing out there in poetry right now, nor the best, nor the most important—I simply think it's happening, and I wanted to call attention to it. One thing I do feel is that there are still not enough ways to approach literature through feminist lenses—multiple feminist lenses!—and my attempt with the Gurlesque was to come up with a new lens colored by my own historic moment and subject position.

Previously I've written the following, in an essay called "On the Gurlesque":

> Well aware that none of the poets I'm discussing sought to be grouped together or thus defined when writing their work, I have struggled with the politics of defining a group that does not seek such definition. I do not want to limit or pigeon-hole these writers or the ways they are read; nonetheless, I find it useful and important to name this phenomenon, because it is spear-headed by young women, and thus in danger of being written out of history, and I seek to validate it by calling attention to it as a real force in contemporary poetry. (par. 20)

Instead of a group or a movement or a school, I see the Gurlesque as a constellation—a subjective but distinctive pattern of individual points of light perceived at a distance. As an aesthetic constellation, I feel that Gurlesque poetry defies categorization: the poets I noticed using its strategies are all over the map in terms of their geographic, ethnic, and educational backgrounds, as well as their poetic lineages. Even within a single poem, Gurlesque poetry can shift from prose to lyric, from ridiculous to sublime, from heartbreaking to ball-busting.

Here are four very different examples of the way Gurlesque poems can employ strategies of hybridity:

You can tell something about the hybrid nature of Geraldine Kim's *Povel* from the title alone: it's not a novel, and not a poem. This book-length text flirts with ideas of what a "girl" literature ought to be, as well as what an Asian-American book ought to be. Its completely original form on the page—strangely positioned sections of quoted passages—underlines its aesthetic excess, practically daring the reader to try and enjoy it: the last section, "WTFJHN"—"what the fuck just happened now"—invites the reader to write their feedback in the book itself, and gives as an example, "This is a piece of shit! I hate this fucking crap it makes no sense how could anyone pay attention to any of this?!" (Kim o)

Likewise, Chelsey Minnis' work, with its extended elliptical phrases (a different, literal use of the "elliptical"!) similarly seems to almost thwart attempts at readings. What to do with all these little dots that connect, or disconnect, the phrases? How to read this punctuation aloud? How to connect with the horrific/baroque/beautiful/goofy text?

In Catherine Wagner's work, the reader is continually having to readjust her lens, because the work feels at once carefully crafted and indebted to traditional verse, while at the same time seems to be falling apart, making a mess, leaving one thought off midway through and embarking on a tangent with no attempt to resolve its parts.

The Flarfist work of Nada Gordon strings together bizarrely girly moments in poems that are as interested in confrontation and low culture as they are in presenting something truly "beautiful" or "meaningful." One of her books is called *V.Imp*, which I love as a Gurlesque title—the conflagration of "very important," high art, ego, the VIP, with something impish, coded, tech-y, weird.

Is such poetry "mainstream"? "Prosey"? "Accessible"? "Experimental"? How does a Flarf poem or *Povel* or Wagner's sung performances fit into such labels?

The Gurlesque certainly owes a lot to the Gothic mode, and it may be useful to recall that in Victorian Gothic lit, a lack of ability to be categorized is what defined the Gothic—the hybrid being as monster, creature, other. Gurlesque *revels* in its otherness, its fluidity, and utilizes it as a way to upend the patrimony of received language, form, and decorum. Gurlesque poetics has the ability to piss off *both* the mainstream and the avant-garde!

But here, of course, is also the problem: is the Gurlesque just another category for the uncategorizable? Is it a way of homogenizing that which resists homogenization? As a Third Wave aesthetic, the Gurlesque is still bound by Second Wave struggles with the patriarchy, and, as it has been smartly pointed out elsewhere, operates on a heterosexual axis, with all the limits this implies. So are we already off the Third Wave and onto a Fourth, which my students like to tell me is one in which the very notion of such gender-bound categories and binaries no longer exist at all? Perhaps this Gurlesque is just a stepping stone towards something even more radical. Perhaps the height of the Gurlesque moment has already peaked. What would a Fourth Wave—a truly borderless—Gurlesque aesthetic look like?

Whitewashing American Hybrid Aesthetics
Craig Santos Perez

Wow. An anthology titled *American Hybrid*. How exciting that the editors wanted to, in the words of David St. John's introduction, "show the historical depth and vitality of the concept of poetic hybridization in American poetry" and to "present the impressive range of poets we believe articulate this impulse" (xxviii).

Certainly the editors would examine the idea of aesthetic hybridity in terms of Native American literature.

Certainly they would cite Arnold Krupat, in *The Voice in the Margin: Native American Literature and the Canon*, who defines indigenous literature as produced "when an author of subaltern cultural identification manages successfully to merge forms internal to his cultural formation with forms external to it" (214).

Or David Murray, in *Forked Tongues: Speech, Writing and Representation in North American Indian Texts*, who sees Native writers "forked" between cultures, languages, oral and written forms, and genres (94).

Or Louis Owens, in *Other Destinies*, who uses the concept of a "mixed-blood" as an aesthetic, experiential, and critical concept. The mixedblood embodies the Native literary text, which is "intensely dialogic, a hybridized narrative within which the author is in dialogue with himself, within which two distinct linguistic consciousnesses, two kinds of discourse, coexist in a 'dialogically agitated and tension-filled environment' " (35).

How many Native American poets are included in this anthology?

Certainly the editors would highlight one of the most cited essays in Asian American literary studies, Lisa Lowe's "Heterogeneity, Hybridity, and Multiplicity," which appeared in her book *Immigrant Acts: On Asian American Cultural Politics*. Lowe defines "hybridity" as "the formation of cultural objects and practices that are produced by the histories of uneven and unsynthetic power relations [. . .] Hybridity, in this sense, does not suggest the assimilation of Asian or immigrant practices to dominant forms but instead marks the history of survival within relationships of unequal power and domination" (67).

Certainly, the editors would cite the extensive theorization of literary hybridity within Latino/a literary studies.

Of course, they would mention Gloria Anzaldúa's *Borderlands/La Frontera: The New Mestiza*, in which she writes: "From the racial, ideological, cultural and biological cross-pollination, an 'alien' consciousness is presently in the making—a new mestiza consciousness, una conciencia de mujer. It is a consciousness of the Borderlands" (77).

Of course, they would mention José David Saldívar's *Border Matters: Remapping American Cultural Studies*. "This zone is the social space of subaltern encounters, the Janus-faced border line in which peoples geopolitically forced to separate themselves now negotiate with one another and manufacture new relations, hybrid cultures, and multiple-voiced aesthetics" (13).

Without a doubt they would include the most important poet/theorist of aesthetic hybridity, Alfred Arteaga, who writes in *Chicano Poetics: Heterotexts and Hybridities*: "The interlingual speech of the Chicano and the hybridized poem in particular are especially apt at expressing the ambiguities inherent in mestizaje and those in either Aztlan or the borderlands. The Chicano's hybrid thought allows for a movement among discourses that replicates the possible range of perspectives on race or the home-land. This speech is interlingual in that it not only acknowledges a confluence of difference but emphasizes the factor of hybridity" (17).

Certainly they would offer a generous selection of work from Guiller-mo Gómez-Peña, El Rey del Híbrido himself.

Is it true that there are no Latino/as in this anthology?

Oops. So much for showing "the historical depth and vitality of the concept of poetic hybridization in American poetry." So much for pre-senting the "impressive range of poets we believe articulate this impulse."

It's easy to be discontent with how this anthology doesn't live up to its title, to be discontent with how incomplete and ignorant it is. There's a fine line between ignorance and prejudice.

But I want to ask: if this is not *truly* an anthology of "American hybrid" poetry and aesthetics, what is it an anthology of?

A clue can be found in the section of Swensen's introduction titled "The Legacy," in which she traces the development of the two-model system in twentieth-century American poetry (xvii-xxi). Swensen's "Legacy" is a white poetic legacy, a white reading of twentieth-century American poetry. (Of all the anthologies she mentions, not a single one is an anthology of ethnic or native American poetry—which is surprising considering no one fetishizes anthologies more than poets of color.)

Thus it becomes clear that "American Hybrid" should have more accurately titled "White American Hybrid." Despite this, Swensen defines hybrid aesthetics in purely aesthetic terms, as Michael Theune has noted (above), resulting in poems that are "conventional . . . yet complicated," "recognizably experimental . . . yet follow[ing] . . . strict formal rules," etc. Why are white poet editors jumping on the hybrid bandwagon so late in the game, seemingly without any true understanding of the his-torical depth and vitality, as well as the complex problematics, of the concept of poetic hybridization in American poetry? Why are they doing this without understanding how whiteness influences this choice?

In my opinion, white poets want to be hybrid for two reasons. One: white poets don't want to be New Critical Fugitive Southern Agrarians "taking their stand" against America's move towards the urban, national, international, industrial, and integrative progress within a self-contained, insular, united, and banded expression of a confederate aesthetic.

Two: white poets don't want to be Kenneth Goldsmith hoarding and molding the provisional disorienting detritus of digital empty signifiers cut, pasted, skimmed, forwarded, spammed, and downloaded into unboring, uncreative writing without allegiance to anyone's "Reality."

Personally, I wouldn't mind being a New Critic—most of them had stable teaching jobs in the academy. I also wouldn't mind being Kenneth Goldsmith; he has cool fedoras and memorable facial hair.

Alas, I am not white so I can't be either. But I feel for all you white poets out there stuck between Southern Rock and a shard of non-place.

I blame Ron Silliman. For many things, but most of all for propagating the simplistic binary reading of poetic history into quietude & avant garde. Let's face it: it's Silliman's poetry world and we just blog in it.

Of course, Silliman solved this binary long ago...by becoming Silliman. But most white poets don't want to be Silliman, either, which I don't understand because he gets tons of free books! Anyway, Silliman forced white writers into the binary of Ransom or Goldsmith, creating white cultural-aesthetic anxiety, which necessitated the formation of an "ideal hybrid," the publication of a white American hybrid anthology, and the establishment of this panel.

However, I must thank Silliman because if this panel didn't exist I wouldn't have gotten funding from my university to attend AWP!

Regardless, in conclusion: white hybrid aesthetics is the rejection of becoming Ransom, becoming Goldsmith, or becoming Silliman.

A Drag Queen's Lament: Or, how I learned to stop worrying and love my camp
Megan Volpert

A hybrid is a new car that may look much the same as your old car, but runs on a fuel that is better for the environment. Also, nine out of ten hybrid car drivers are certifiably smug. Despite the warm fuzzy feeling of superiority provided by the notion of hybridity, the practical fact remains that many of these cars accelerate unpredictably or have no functioning brake system. The automotive and poetry industries have these things in common. In the case of poetics, are the heralds of hybridity justifiably optimistic about their claims? The rhetoric of poetic hybridity suffers the same operational faults as hybrid cars, but there is likely light at the end of our tunnel.

To find it, we will need a gay agenda. The rhetoric and practical politics of sexuality is in many ways a historical parallel to hybridity. To begin with, in true drag queen fashion, we will present evidence in the form of an object of ridicule. Let us succumb to an obvious choice, the Toyota Prius of poetics—*American Hybrid: A Norton Anthology of New Poetry*. We will try to overlook the fact that when Norton releases an anthology in your honor, it means your cutting edge has officially been dulled. My apologies to Cole Swensen, as this is an obvious and tired target. And as a sidebar, apologies to David St. John for leaving his preface almost entirely out of this discussion; we'll only come back to his two pages of vague sentiment for a moment, after sinking our teeth into Cole's ten pages of historical specificity.

In the first section of her preface, Swensen outlines the legacy of American poetry as essentially a two-camp model and concludes by saying that poetries are so fragmented now that it is no longer possible to properly identify them by the labels of the old camps. This is akin to bisexuals and transpeople giving folks who identify merely as "homosexual" something to think about. In the face of problematic boundaries, we are forced to look into broader descriptive terminology. Thusly: the "third way" labels of queer and hybrid.

The second section of Swensen's preface argues that hybridity draws the old system of camps to a close. Sure, if history has taught us nothing. Here's that lovely Derridian trick where oppositionality necessarily constructs a fresh binary. Different rhetoric, same dichotomous logic: if you don't think hybridity is the next big thing, you must be defending the tired old thing. But the good people of San Francisco do not stop wearing their little colored bandana fetish markers just because they've become one nation under queerness.

"Hybrid" is an umbrella term that points to the problem of camps; it does not eliminate camps. For example, Swensen refers to Barbara

Guest as "the quintessential hybrid poet" (xxii). Was she not the quint-essential New York School poet? Oh, there were subtle differences; she was marginalized by those poets. But then what is John Ashbery doing in the table of contents? Also, almost every poet included in this anthol-ogy is over forty years old. I thought the subtitle said this was an anthol-ogy of "new poetry." So this is what people are complaining about: that the Norton anthology is recycling. That it's not the new car; it's the old car with a new paint job. That the gas mileage remains what it was.

And by "gas mileage," I mean "marketability." In the final section of Swensen's preface, she says that two-camp hierarchies are out and frag-mentary hubs are in. She even goes so far as to say "the rhizome is an appropriate model" (xxv). But let us read into Deleuze and Guattari further—enough to reveal that these rhizomes are bound to get picked off one at a time, co-opted back into the system of dichotomies that has (dis)served us so well. So, we now return to the joke about the Norton anthology. People are saying this anthology doesn't represent for "the real hybridity," the exciting stuff happening in our own moment. Nor-ton's co-option of the hybridity label (represented by the popular attacks on this anthology) proves that hybridity is becoming mainstream (and therefore increasingly acceptable in the practical world of the market-place) in the way that queer has likewise become acceptable.

So it's true that this is not a compendium of small press findings, or of internet pings, or of fresh young voices. This is not holding up leather-clad drag queens as a glimmering possibility of the future, but good old Colonel Margaret Cammermeyer, tried and true. This is basi-cally a selection of poets whose work and influence has for the most part long been accepted either as the mainstream or at least by the mainstream. Oh, but they never received appropriate critical recognition in their moment. Well, cry me a river for poor John Ashbery!

Who among us would not gladly sacrifice a limb to be considered half so seriously and thoroughly as most of the poets in this anthology have already been? This is the drag queens getting jealous that they are not on the cover of *Time Magazine* like the nice, white lesbian couple who simply long to adopt a baby into their stable suburban home. Envy in this case is essentially a symptom of the willingness to be co-opted, to be recognized and assimilated into the mainstream as represented by the Norton anthology—a symptom of the joys of "selling out," of your own rhizome coming up on the radar of The Borg.

According to Deleuze and Guattari, this co-option is to a certain extent good because it enables us to become spies in the enemy camp. We can work some changes from the inside, and as the old saying goes, use the master's tools to dismantle the master's house. Acceptability in the language provokes acceptability for the idea itself, which eventually leads to real political change. But then (ouch!) the glass ceiling: queers can keep jobs but still can't get married; hybrid poets can publish in online zines but none of us new kids got published in the classy Norton anthology.

In reference to queerness, D. A. Miller calls this "the open secret." Hybridity is here, but hybrid poets—the new kids—have not yet arrived (i.e., been afforded the luxury of selling out). Of all the poets excluded by the editors' decision to restrict consideration to only those poets with three books published by 2005, St. John says, "I can only add that their anthology is yet to come" (xxviii). Should we already be humbling ourselves to the label of "second generation hybrid poets," thanks to the Norton anthology?

Visibility is the driving force of social change. If we don't notice it's broke, we're not going to fix it. To dig back into the history of contemporary poetics and find or reveal hybridity by reclassifying the older folks as hybrid, rather than avant-garde, or postmodern, or experimental or whathaveyou, accomplishes one major thing: an apology. On the political stage that is our marketplace, "hybridity" is a label that we have so far safely slapped only on poets whose work appears to have been overlooked in their moment in some way. Previously, we thought it was weird, or shocking, or we just didn't get it. It was hideously homosexual, like a public service announcement about pedophiles.

You know hybridity when you see it, but you only see it in retrospect? In the glory of hindsight, we apologize to these folks and renegotiate the history of our critical lens to turn them into pioneers. They are the drag queens at Stonewall—pretty controversial at the time. We re-vision, so as to feel less guilty for not having properly or entirely recognized all the facets of their genius when these poets first showed it to us. Sorry we let the paddy wagons cart you off to jail, you loud and obnoxious drag queens, but here's a belated thank you for saving our bar that night. So the anniversary of the Stonewall riot is widely considered to mark the beginning of the gay liberation era. But then (ouch!) please don't show up to our Pride parade this summer, if you plan to embarrass us with vulgar displays that the media will then air as a representation of our totality. Only our best foot forward, please.

In the third section of her preface, Swensen cites feminism, multiculturalism, and translation as forces of movement toward hybridity. Though we now mostly consider these elements an unavoidable given, once upon a time, the mainstream establishment also considered them to be a shameful pain in the ass. When last we tuned in, these were forces of movement toward postmodernism. Ah, postmodernism: a movement that probably had the worst public relations campaign in the whole history of ideas. Is there a difference between postmodernism and hybridity? Tired of the unmarketability of "postmodernism," are we just giving the car a fresh paint job? What is the point of this new label, "hybridity"?

Indeed: "postmodernism" is a loud and obnoxious drag queen, while "hybridity" is two middle-class mommies on the cover of *Time Magazine*. It certainly has not yet helped us—the new kids—publish more respectably, win more recognition, or find a bigger audience for our work. It has not pioneered any concepts, but simply rehashes those that since 1945 have been going by so many other names. So what is there to be smug about? That's not smugness—it's the grimace of pain that comes with having jammed your foot in the door just before it closes.

So now, what rough beast slouches toward hybridity, waiting to be born? Where is the poet we can smuggle in under the rhetoric of hybridity? Where is the poem for which we have jammed our foot in the door? We are waiting for the barbarians, right? As students of history, we know that it is better to use the lessons of the past in order to work toward a smarter future, as opposed to just revising the past and writing a new history. Revisionism alone is not enough. Let us be forward-thinking, on the ball enough to admit that we need the mainstreaminess of the Norton anthology to make the language of hybridity happen, but now those on the ground behind enemy lines have practical work to do. This is a foot in the door for drag queens.

I would like to suggest that the new movement, and perhaps the only movement forthcoming in our future (though its motley crew of practitioners would probably not like to be called a "movement") is a coalition of the willing also known as: the unapologetic. Deleuze and Guattari would get a big bang out of this future. It is a future where we will not apologize to the poets of the past for our inability or disinterest in recognizing their talents to a fuller extent. We will not apologize for being beyond or within the mainstream, or establishment, or usual suspects of marginal politics, or predictable indicators of marketability. We will not apologize for the problem of all our labels and no labeling system adequate to classify us. We will not apologize to this or that camp for our own campiness. We're here, we're unapologetic, get used to it.

To summarize, as a type of identity politics, we can evaluate the effectiveness of "hybridity" as a labeling system in comparison to previous labeling systems, such as the notion of "avant-garde." Or, we in the world of marginal sexual politics used to call ourselves LGBT, but in this increasingly broad field of weirdness that is the having of body and sexuality, that long string of acronyms has given way to one beautifully simplistic catch-all. So "hybrid" is the new "queer." If we view hybridity as ontology rather than simply as ideology (that is, what it aspires to be, rather than only what it has so far said), we will discover that hybridity is only the rose of the avant-garde by another name, and this is not bad.

Hybridity has yet not been truly transformative, but instead faces the same operational pitfalls as avant-gardism. This is because, essentially, what we've been doing is a kind of incrementalism, a pragmatic approach to poetic civil liberties. Nobody takes umbrage with John Ashbery anymore, so put Ashbery on the cover of *Time Magazine* as the poster child for the movement, and people will find it palatable. People will even teach it to undergrads—thanks, Norton. And so returning now to vague sentiment, we can echo St. John's idyllic conclusion, "let the gates of the Garden stand open" (xxviii). Eventually, though it is slow-going and meanwhile cause for jealous catfights, there should be room on the bookshelf for all of us, drag queens included.

Works Referenced

Burt, Stephen. *Close Calls with Nonsense: Reading New Poetry*. St. Paul, MN: Graywolf, 2009. Print.

Caplan, David. *Questions of Possibility: Contemporary Poetry and Poetic Form*. Oxford: Oxford UP, 2005. Print.

Finch, Annie, and Katherine Varnes, eds. *An Exaltation of Forms: Contemporary Poets Celebrate the Diversity of Their Art*. Ann Arbor: U of Michigan P, 2002. Print.

Fulton, Alice. *Feeling as a Foreign Language: The Good Strangeness of Poetry*. St. Paul, MN: Graywolf, 1999. Print.

Glenum, Lara, and Arielle Greenberg, eds. *Gurlesque: The New Grrly, Grotesque, Burlesque Poetics*. Ardmore, PA: Saturnalia, 2010. Print.

Gordon, Nada. *V.Imp*. Newton, MA: Faux, 2002. Print.

Minnis, Chelsey. *Zirconia*. New York: Fence, 2001. Print.

———. *Bad, Bad*. New York: Fence, 2007. Print.

Noto, John. "Response to the Postmoderns (and Post-Punkers!)." *Talisman* 11 (1993): 183-191. Print.

The Plumbline School. theplumblineschool.blogspot.com. Web.

Poetry 194.4 (July/August 2009). Print.

Rankine, Claudia, and Juliana Spahr, eds. *American Women Poets in the 21st Century: Where Lyric Meets Language*. Middletown, CT: Wesleyan UP, 2002. Print.

Renek, Nava, ed. *Wreckage of Reason: An Anthology of Contemporary Xxperimental Prose by Women Writers*. New York: Spuyten Duyvil, 2008. Print.

Shepherd, Reginald. *The Iowa Anthology of New American Poetries*. Iowa City, IA: U of Iowa P, 2004. Print.

———. *Lyric Postmodernisms: An Anthology of Contemporary Innovative Poetries*. Denver, CO: Counterpath, 2008. Print.

Swensen, Cole, and David St. John, eds. *American Hybrid: A Norton Anthology of New Poetry*. New York: Norton, 2009. Print.

Theune, Michael. "Missed Communication: Three New Anthologies." *Pleiades* 29.2 (2009): 186-212. Print.

Wagner, Cathy. *Macular Hole*. New York: Fence, 2004. Print.

———. *Miss America*. New York: Fence, 2001. Print.

Wallace, Mark and Steven Marks, eds. *Telling It Slant: Avant Garde Poetics of the 1990s*. Tuscaloosa, AL: U of Alabama P, 2001. Print.

Works Cited

Anzaldúa, Gloria. *Borderlands/La Frontera: The New Mestiza*. San Francisco: Aunt Lute, 1987. Print.

Arteaga, Alfred. *Chicano Poetics: Heterotexts and Hybridities*. Cambridge: Cambridge UP, 1997. Print.

Burt, Stephen. "Close Calls with Nonsense: How to Read, and Perhaps Enjoy, Very New Poetry." *Close Calls with Nonsense: Reading New Poetry*. St. Paul, MN: Graywolf, 2009. 5-19. Print.

Eliot, T. S. "Andrew Marvell." *Selected Essays, 1917-1932*. New York: Harcourt, 1932. 251-63. Print.

Gioia, Dana. "Can Poetry Matter?" *Can Poetry Matter: Essays on Poetry and American Culture*. St. Paul, MN: Graywolf, 1992. 1-21. Print.

Göransson, Johannes. "american hybrid review." *Exoskeleton*. 02 Aug. 2009. Web. 15 Jan. 2010.

———. "Nonsense/Burt/Hybrid." *Exoskeleton*. 29 Apr. 2009. Web. 15 Mar. 2010.

Greenberg, Arielle. "On the Gurlesque." *Small Press Traffic: News & Reports*. 8 Jan. 2004. Web. 1 Mar. 2010.

Kim, Geraldine. *Povel*. New York: Fence, 2005. Print.

Krupat, Arnold. *The Voice in the Margin: Native American Literature and the Canon*. Berkeley: U of California P, 1989. Print.

Lowe, Lisa. *Immigrant Acts: On Asian American Cultural Politics*. Durham, NC: Duke UP, 1996. Print.

Murray, David. *Forked Tongues: Speech, Writing and Representation in North American Indian Texts*. Bloomington, IN: Indiana UP, 1991. Print.

Owens, Louis. *Other Destinies: Understanding the American Indian Novel*. Norman: U of Oklahoma P, 1992. Print.

Powell, D. A. "dogs and boys can treat you like trash. and dogs do love trash." *Cocktails*. St. Paul, MN: Graywolf, 2004. 14. Print.

Saldívar, José David. *Border Matters: Remapping American Cultural Studies*. Berkeley: U of California P, 1997. Print.

Shepherd, Reginald. "Introduction." *Lyric Postmodernisms: An Anthology of Contemporary Innovative Poetries*. Ed. Reginald Shepherd. Denver, CO: Counterpath, 2008. xi-xvii. Print.

———. "One State of the Art." *Pleiades: A Journal of New Writing*. 27.1 (2007): 2-10. Print.

Silliman, Ron. *Silliman's Blog*. 18 Feb. 2010. Web. 15 Mar. 2010. Web.

Smith, Barbara Herrnstein. *Poetic Closure: A Study of How Poems End*. Chicago: U of Chicago P, 1968. Print.

Smith, Clark Ashton. "The Dark Eidolon." *The Colossus of Ylourgne and Three Others*. Rockville, MD: Wildside, 2009. 13-35. Print.

St. John, David. "Introduction." *American Hybrid: A Norton Anthology of New Poetry*. Ed. Cole Swensen and David St. John. New York: Norton, 2009. xxvii-xxviii. Print.

Swensen, Cole. "Introduction." *American Hybrid: A Norton Anthology of New Poetry*. Ed. Cole Swensen and David St. John. New York: Norton, 2009. xvii-xxvi. Print.

Response to "Hybrid Aesthetics and Its Discontents"

Cole Swensen

I would like to thank the editors of this volume for giving me the opportunity to add a few words here, for though, of course, many things are covered in these papers, the *American Hybrid* anthology is referred to sufficiently frequently and in the context of such crucial issues, that, as one of its editors, I value the chance to join the conversation, even after the fact. The anthology project was, for me, far from unfraught with many of the concerns addressed in these papers. I felt it was worth risking them because I hoped that what would be gained, particularly in terms of bringing many people's work before a larger public, would be worth the inevitable difficulties and disagreements. Megan Volpert remarks that these people are all already well-known, but I think that, while it might seem so to a deeply committed, deeply involved poet, in fact, a good many of the people in the volume are not known at all beyond that deeply committed, but small, world. I found all the papers here extremely interesting and agree with much of what is said in all of them. I particularly valued Michael Theune's observations about the lack of humor—it's really true—and a lack! And I hear very seriously Craig Santos Perez's criticism—the anthology he implies that ours should have been, while a different project entirely, would make a wonderful book, and I hope someone does it soon.

One of the general concerns raised here repeatedly about *American Hybrid* and, to some degree, Reginald Shepherd's *Lyric Postmodernisms,* is that it tends to minimize differences and seems to be trying to make a case for a homogeneous middle ground. The rationale for the AWP panel is a case in point, stating, "Such synthesizing aesthetics are ubiquitous in American poetry." This conflates synthesizing and hybridizing, disregarding their important distinction: in a hybrid, the heterogeneous elements remain distinct; in a synthesis, they do not. Another example is the title of Mark Wallace's paper, "Against Unity," as well as much of its content, such as the statement, "This notion of hybrid tries to find similarity across divergent practices. It breaks down the idea of singular schools by looking for things different poetic groups have in common. It tries to find middle ground. It imagines itself, perhaps, as a new center, one from which the most extreme and divisive elements of divergent practices have been tempered or simply removed." I'm amazed by this statement—it's simply an inaccurate reading of the *American Hybrid* anthology, ignoring and even directly contradicting what is expressly stated in the introduction and imputing to its editors values and agenda that we simply don't hold. We are not trying to find similarities, or a middle ground; we have no desire whatsoever to remove divisive and divergent practices—in fact, we present quite a few in the anthology—and the only time I used the term "center" to speak of the work was in the phrase "a center of alterity," specifically to figure any assumed center as itself a collection of differences.

Nowhere in the introduction or other framing materials is the word "synthesis" or "synthesize" used, nor the word "unity," nor any word that would suggest unity; instead, difference is repeatedly stressed. The first paragraph of the introduction posits that "everywhere we find complex aesthetic and ideological differences; the contemporary moment is dominated by rich writings that cannot be categorized." Page xx repeats the stress on difference: "American poetry finds itself at a moment when idiosyncrasy rules to such a degree and differences are so numerous that distinct factions are hard, even impossible, to pin down." And the introduction ends on a note stressing difference: "Poetry is eternally marked by, even determined by, difference, but that very difference changes and moves. At the moment, it is moving inside, into the center of the writing itself, fissuring its smooth faces into fragments that make us reconsider the ethics of language, on the one hand, and redraft our notions of a whole, on the other." And the rest of the paragraph goes on to develop the argument that the operative differences of today are found within the writings themselves rather than among poetic communities.

In short, the point that I would most like to stress, and that I thought was made strongly enough in the anthology's introduction, but may be the sort of point that simply can't be made strongly enough without making it several times, is that we are not proposing the work in the anthology as a single thing or even a "thing" in any way. Such a model, while offering an easy way to talk about the work, would have run counter to our whole point, and cannot work for an anthology such as this in which the various poets' works have many more differences than they have similarities. About the only thing the poets in *American Hybrid* have in common—and this is clearly stated—is what they *don't* do—and that is to adhere to or uphold either of the dominant camps of 1960 to 1990 American poetry— and yet (and it is another common, and organizing, point) they come out of environments in which that binary model was a principle influence, and they have chosen to rethink it, often with results that leave them outside the available poetic labels, be they two, five, or fifty.

Furthermore, we did not and do not claim that this breakdown of the binary model is the only thing, or even the principle thing, though I do think it's an important thing, going on in American poetry today. In fact, we did the opposite; for both of us, the "A" in the subtitle "*A Norton anthology of new poetry*" was crucial. It does not claim to be *The,* but rather one of a number of possible configurations of or lenses on contemporary American poetry. It doesn't presume to address all that is happening in American poetry today, particularly those many aspects that don't come out of that binary tradition.

Much contemporary work that is politically-based, that is performance-based, orally-based, or conceptually-based, and much work that has roots in cultures and languages other than American English, isn't in this volume because it developed outside the influence of the two-camp post-1960 model that forms the point of departure for the anthology, and so isn't an aspect of the particular question it addresses. Such work is part of other, equally important and promising questions, many of which have their own recent anthologies in which much of the work in *American Hybrid* would not be appropriate. To ask an anthology to be inclusive of an entire moment in a culture as large and varied as that of the U.S. is, I think, unrealistic and unwise. For one, it's an impossible task, but even more, such an attempt would obliterate the lines of development, of influence and response, that give any cultural product its distinctive shape. As Craig Santos Perez says ("Swensen defines hybrid aesthetics in purely aesthetic terms"), it is a selection based on aesthetic criteria, and on specific, historically-determined aesthetic criteria that is clearly identified. This is not to suggest that aesthetics can ever be divorced from social, political, ethical, philosophical, and other sorts of concerns, or that aesthetic choices don't have political and social repercussions, but that, just as one can use a social or political or philosophical orientation as the selective criterion of an anthology, one can use an aesthetic one as well; such a move does not deny the validity of other orientations.

None of the readers of any anthology are actually there for the process of its construction, which is a loss, though an inevitable one, as much of what an anthology might offer is most alive in the discussions, the decisions, the distinctions, and the evolving considerations that lead to what ends up being the tip of an iceberg—the final selections, ordering, and framing that become the anthology itself. In this case, when we started the project, David and I thought that we would be presenting more younger people and not so many of the generation currently over sixty. But as we got to looking closely at lots and lots of work, I kept finding myself thinking of the roots of the innovations I was reading, and it caused me to go back to earlier voices whose echoes I was hearing, and to listen to them differently—which often amounted to hearing them detached from the presumptions of their literary affiliations. It was a case in which the work of younger people gave us a new view of that of some older poets, and, increasingly, it was this view that we wanted to present because it marks an historically important shift in American poetry.

There is an unarticulated but pervasive prejudice in American culture that only the young can be innovators; Megan Volpert sums it up well by saying "every poet included in this anthology is over forty years old. I thought the subtitle said this was an anthology of 'new poetry.'" Such a statement confuses the words "young" and "new" and implies that only the young can do anything new, which consigns people to history much too quickly and ignores the fact that people who are great innovators in their twenties and thirties tend to keep on being so all their lives. This prejudice also encourages cultural products—and their creators—to be regarded as consumables with the same expected obsolescence as seasonal fashions or computers. We wanted to present writers who are exactly such life-long innovators; some of them are by now the masters to which younger poets look—and they look to them not only for what they did in and for certain recognizable groups, but above all for the ways in which they have continued changing and have moved beyond familiar labels into their own idiosyncratic territories.

What we perceived in the work of both older and younger writers was poetry that crossed and confused the line dividing the experimental from the conventional, a line that created an oppositional model that is in itself excruciatingly reductive. But we are not proposing to replace that binary with a unity—quite the opposite. The work gathered in the *American Hybrid* anthology is not a collapsing-towards-the-middle, not a center-between-extremes, but is exactly the contrary; each poet's work is a different deviation from the linear continuum that runs from the conventional to the experimental; taken together, they form an errant field that explodes that narrow, linear path into a three dimensional space in which the unique nature of each body of work is discernable, and tidy groupings are difficult or impossible to make.

On a less general level, criticism has reached me concerning two aspects about which I felt, and still feel, extremely strongly—the equal number of pages allotted to each poet and the alphabetical organization—so I am going to take the opportunity to state why we chose them in case the reasoning behind these choices might offer some people a way to think about them differently.

Choosing the poets and the poems is a strong statement of opinion in itself. We had a very hard time narrowing down the poets, and there were so many more that we wanted to include that we had no wish to impose or imply any further hierarchy of value by allotting some more space than others. All the poets here, we feel, are excellent and interesting and more than deserving of the space we were able to give them; readers are free to make their own distinctions regarding those more or less important to them. To offer fewer than five or six pages of a poet's work does not give readers sufficient material to make such distinctions and cannot give any sense of the work's scope. This anthology presented particular challenges in that several of the writers use page-space in crucial ways that the Norton format could not accommodate and that made the re-formatted length difficult to predict. Any difference in the length of the selections is due to that; ideally, they would have all been identical to the millimeter.

We ordered the writers alphabetically in order to avoid creating new schools or factions out of what we perceived as the erosion of two principal ones, and any way of grouping these poets other than the most arbitrary—any grouping based on perceived affinities of style, principles, or background, or even based on age or geography—seemed to do just that. I specifically wanted each writer to be taken as much on her or his own terms as logistically possible, and refusing to construct lines of demarcation among them seemed to address that.

Some anthologies try to predict emerging tendencies, try to spotlight what the future will consider historically important, which is a gesture that also helps to create just what it's claiming to discern. Donald Allen's anthology did that, and did it marvelously well. Other anthologies celebrate work that has already been accomplished. We chose the latter approach because we felt we were seeing something important in the structure and impetus for change in American poetry that had already occurred and wasn't getting sufficiently acknowledged, that was, instead, getting subsumed under an outdated "tradition/experiment" dichotomy, whose strong sway tended (and still tends, in some places) to obscure other, subtler currents. Despite Mark Wallace's enumeration of various distinct groupings, and his perceptive and accurate description of them, I find there remains an us/them mentality that obscures the actual intricacy of this one part of the contemporary American poetry map. Our desire was to get beyond that us/them mentality in order to look at a specific body of work in more complex ways—and in going beyond that, to engage in analyses and identities that are not based on opposition, that do not require the negation of an other in order to figure.

Goodbye, Goodbye, Goodbye:
Notes on the Ends of Poems

Joy Katz

O ur feel for endings comes from stories, movies, sports—all of our cultural underpinnings. "That's All, Folks!" rang out every night, nudging us toward the dinner table. At the end of the fourth quarter the winning team rushes the goal posts. We usually don't wonder whether to turn the last page when we read novels. If we are left hanging—"to be continued" is satisfying in its own way—we know the next episode is coming. Jokes have punch lines. Television commercials have logos. Symphonies crescendo. At the end of her floor exercise, the gymnast springs into a "Y" shape. Cool and serve with whipped cream. Roll credits.

Poems have their own kinds of endings. Most of the time, and even when a poem is deliberately "unfinished," a reader expects nothing more than the white space on the page after the last line. This "absence of further continuation," as Barbara Herrnstein Smith says in her classic book on the subject, *Poetic Closure*, is a crucial presence in a poem. A piece ought to end well if we are to feel we have made something or read a complete utterance.

But a really fine ending need not be a stock ending, or even feel like an ending as we know it. (William Carlos Williams complained that too many poems click like a box.) As an editor, as well as a judge and screener of manuscripts, I read a lot of poems. What I see seems to suggest that, at this moment, there aren't as many ways to finish poems as there are to start them. This essay comprises an investigation—perhaps interrogation is a better word—of the kind of ending I see most often, a few ideas about when and how to try something else, and, for inspiration, a collection of alternative endings.

* * *

Pick up any current journal, or just about any book written in the past ten or fifteen years, and you'll notice a lot of repetition in the last two or three lines of poems whose principal mode is not repetition (i.e., poems that aren't ghazals or villanelles, for instance). Here are the last lines from three different poems in a journal pulled randomly from a stack on my desk:

> Then so we now all drink it—drink it all.
> Soldier, drink my blood to rise and live. (Scott 97)

> It melts because it melts, and melts fast because it
> once was hard, once the opposite of us. (Kercheval 156)

> And to be old, and to be dirty, and to be dead—
> O, ladies, ladies. (Scott 107)

On one hand, these three endings are different. The first poem closes with a command: someone orders a soldier to drink. The second ends by offering an explanation. X happens because of y. The third creates closure by giving death the last word. It's a time-honored strategy: think of all the movies, operas, and plays that end with death. The endings have different structures, yet all contain repeating tropes: drink/drink/drink, melts/melts/melts, once/once, to be/to be/to be. Lots of poems do the same. Here are five ends-of-poems from *The Best American Poetry 2009*:

> Two black oars angle up from the waves, and the oarsman waits.
>   (Mackowski 79)
> . . . *I can't hear you, I can't hear you.* (Friman 26)
> Gray fox and gray fox. Red, red, red. (Oliver 94)
> Palm fronds clatter and shift in the porous light: clockwise; counter-
>   clockwise. (Sutton 124)

But what of the mice? Where have the mice gone? (Yee 147)

... and a few from the anthology *The New Young American Poets*:

You remember it later: its eye
like a button,
a button on another person's coat. (Ansel 4)

And every other groove) a horn's valved pose.
Asked for, asked for, asked for. (Ellis 59)

And she used the very pointed tip of her tongue.
(That tongue, O, that tongue.) (Parker 136)

not with the compass, *not* with the map. (Volkman 179)

Again, the poems come to their ends by various means: a song that brings to mind a nursery rhyme ("gray fox and gray fox . . ."); a shift to a different subject, in the form of a question ("where have the mice gone?"); and an image of movement that continues outside the timeframe of the poem (the shifting palm fronds). The second batch includes a leap to a later time, a negative insistence (the italic pair of "nots"), a slip into ecstasy with "O." But all the poems repeat themselves as they close.

Even as I write this sentence, more poems are flipping their alligator tails back and forth. In a brand-new book on my desk, twenty-two of sixty-two poems, or more than a third, end with the repeating trope. In another fairly recent collection, in the Yale Younger Poets series, fifteen of twenty-one poems sign off with repetition.

Reiteration is everywhere, including at the close of prose poems—

... to its maleficent greed, to its splintered breath and carnal haste.
(Lehmann)

... That, and how anybody can just lie down and make an angel, even
a Tartar. Even an angel. (Lerner 13)

—and in the last lines of not only lyrics and narratives but also more difficult and disjunctive poems:

The cupboard is bare. Me, me, me, I don't care. (Bang 39)

In the next street, a boy walked alone, counting the cobblestones:
One, one, one, one, one. (Swensen 18)

... and myself, too proudly proud. (Sharma 4)

I am not suggesting that the repeating trope is bad. On the contrary. One of the reasons so many poets use repetition as that it is fulfilling. As Herrnstein Smith notes, its force is an essential part of literature (31). Repetition as closure also is not new. The pattern goes back at least to the Middle Ages and the troubadours. When *Poetic Closure* was published, in 1968, Herrnstein Smith found the repeating ending "most common in poetry [that] retains its connection to primitive or naïve sources" (31). In American poetry now, though, the repetitive sign-off has become increasingly common among all kinds of poems. Here I am using it in my own first book:

> . . . and you, reader, can you get out of the poem?
> By not finishing, by turning the page? (Katz 42)

I might as well have been questioning the purpose of this particular contemporary poetic ending, because it is starting to seem more a convention than a choice. Why do we use it so often? Do we repeat because of an unconsciously imagined expectation on the part of the reader? Are poems with such endings wired to trigger the admiring "ohhh" response at readings? Are all these endings-with-repetition trap doors we use to get out of the poem when we don't know how else to do it? Are they just habit?

There is no single answer. But as this catalogue of endings suggests, one reason we repeat is because we repeat. If you read any amount of poetry, you have probably grown used to hearing words repeated at the end of a poem, so you may turn to the goodbye, goodbye ending more often than you realize. Second, the ear loves repetition. A poem is perhaps most like song when it repeats. And then, naturally, there is tradition. Our reiterative endings recall not just the relatively recent past of Ashbery's "My wife / Thinks I'm in Oslo—Oslo, France, that is," or Plath's "In a forest of frost, in a dawn of cornflowers" or, going back further, T. S. Eliot lingering "in the chambers of the sea / By sea-girls wreathed with seaweed red and brown," but also Yeats's "how can we know the dancer from the dance?" Which itself looks back to Keats's "Beauty is truth, truth beauty," but also to the sixteenth century of Sir Philip Sidney's "thy thorn without, my thorn my heart invadeth." Sir Philip, for his part, might have had the end of Shakespeare's Eighteenth Sonnet knocking around in his mind: "So long lives this, and this gives life to thee." Fast-forward to Frost, trudging off down the path: "And miles to go before I sleep. And miles to go before I sleep." And so on. And so on. And so on.

Looking more closely at tradition, though, it might be that our recent poems, most of which are not in received forms, are reaching back to the *security* of tradition as they end. Closural repetition as free-verse form, at least in English. In prose poems, the reiterative ending occasionally seems imported, for familiarity, from lineated verse—prose gesturing toward poetry by way of its ending, when a different, possibly more prose-like, ending might even strengthen the poetics of the piece.

The process of publishing and submitting probably affects the ends of poems, too. Journal editors are chronically short on time and room. When hundreds of poems come in, and an editor can pick just one, she may, unconsciously, pick the one that feels "complete in itself," with an ending that seems like an ending as she knows it. Editors prize innovation, and they don't like to think they have biases. But familiarity surely influences how screeners, especially less experienced screeners, read the slush pile, and it is probably adding to the number of reiterative endings in books and journals. Not that that's a reason to keep to old habits. More a reason editors, readers of submissions, and teachers of workshop should be aware of the ubiquitous final double- and triple-kick.[1]

If you're looking at a draft of a poem that ends with repeating language, it's probably a good idea to question it, or at least be less in love with it. Is there a strong reason for the repetition? Is the poem trotting off or blowing kisses instead of doing something more natural, more interesting, arresting, or unexpected? If the ending feels right because it feels familiar, and it's songlike, is that enough? If you're putting a manuscript together, read the last four lines of every poem in it. If many poems in a book close in the same way, it's like the sound of the same door shutting,

---

1. A survey of books written by poets outside the Academy, rather than by poets who teach in MFA programs, might be interesting. A recent Walt Whitman Award winner, by a poet who teaches in the public schools, included only seven reiterative endings among fifty-nine poems. I like to think poetry workshops have many more benefits than drawbacks, depending, but poets in them do catch tropes from each other—not that that is always a bad thing, either.

in the same way, over and over.[2] Perhaps some of the poems could leap to a different place, stagger across the line, or be left open.

You can test the ending by eliminating the repetition. "... Never mind what you asked of me," for example, is better than "... Never mind what you asked, and in your asking said." A stronger ending also might be hovering two or three lines earlier. Finding the natural end of a poem is sometimes like snapping off an asparagus stem where it breaks naturally. Poems can strain toward repetition, shouting *FIN*, when an unstudied conclusion is elsewhere on the page. You can also try moving the end of the poem to the beginning and see what happens. (Far fewer free-verse poems begin with repetition than end with it.)

You might discover the poem wants a different ending altogether. The end of a poem need not be end-of-the-poemlike. Poems can end *in medias res*, with an interruption, an ellipsis, a change of subject, and still feel satisfying. Here are several examples.

Ways to End Other Than By Repeating

I. A POSTMODERN JUMP CUT. Robert Hass's prose poem "Vintage," part narrative, part meditation, has not one but three endings.

At the beginning of the poem a couple is strolling through Greenwich Village, eating deli salads and talking about life. Hass cuts from small- to large-scale images—chicken salad, a grand landscape of mountains—and from intimate ideas, such as watching movies in childhood, to the Big Idea of suffering. Ten stanzas in, the couple encounters a disabled man selling pencils, and the poem offers the first of its possible endings:

> Would the good Christ of Manhattan have restored his sight and two thirds of his left leg? Or would he have healed his heart and left him there in a mutilated body? And what would that peace feel like? (6)

What would the white space on the page feel like if these were the last lines of the poem? To close by proposing that Christ might have brought further suffering along with his good intentions would be to close on a

---

2. Poems written as part of extended sequences, or a book-length project, may be under less pressure to click shut or end with repeating tropes. As with chapter books or television episodes, there is something that came before, and something coming next, so less weight rests on the ending of any single poem.

Big Moment. The stanza sounds like an ending, but its strategy is more Charles Wright[3] than Robert Hass. Closing on the abstract question would be out of scale with this poem, and it doesn't fit with Hass's gentle, ruminative voice and his sense of humor. Instead, the poem goes on:

> It makes you want, at this point, a quick cut, or a reaction shot. "The taxis rivered up Sixth Avenue." "A little sunlight touched the steeple of the First Magyar Reform Church." (6)

It's easy to imagine ending here, at the penultimate stanza. That would be closing on image, a different poetic tradition. The cabs and the lovely steeple distract us from the panhandler. But the poem itself concedes the strategy is hollow. You can't feel better by averting your gaze. "It makes you want," Hass says, acknowledging his own craving—a modernist craving—for redemption by way of an image. But the steeple merely exists alongside the suffering, the way Mary's beatific face hangs above Jesus's in the *pietà*. The poem then circles back to the scene in the West Village.

> In fact, the clerk in the liquor store was appalled. "No, no," he said, "that cabernet can't be drunk for another five years." (6)

"No, no!"—a cinematic cut to the liquor store lets even the clerk disdain the comforting yellow cabs. The true conclusion takes pressure off the poem, too, letting it exist as a conversation on a walk rather than a troubled thrust into imponderables.

2. A CHANGE OF FORM AND DICTION. Theodore Roethke was a depressive, an alcoholic, a sad man. But the pleasure of his poem "The Longing" is the way it veers suddenly from sadness to delight and wonder, especially as it concludes. The poem leads *North American Sequence*, a series of meditations on death and transcendence written near the end of the poet's life. Like almost all of Roethke's poems, it is steeped in the natural world: leaves, rivers, fish, the "castoreum of mink or weasels." But it's also alive with "saliva dripping from warm microphones" and the "agony of crucifixion on barstools." Compared with gulls, who have a job—circling over garbage—poets are essentially purposeless. Roethke can only ever be an observer. It's a role as meaningful as a blind shoot off a potato: "To this

---

3. "No footbridge or boat over Lethe, / No staircase or stepping-stone / up into the Into." Charles Wright, *Sestets*. Farrar, Straus and Giroux, 2009: p. 42.

extent I'm a stalk," Roethke says. A wretched stalk, but then, in the next lines: "how free, how all alone. Out of these nothings /—All beginnings come."

In the final stanza, Roethke, longing for a way out of exasperation, longing for solace, suddenly invents a different future for himself. It's a pure flight of fancy, a piece of advice from the beyond, expressed as if by a little boy:

> Old men should be explorers?
> I'll be an Indian.
> Ogalala?
> Iroquois. (15)

The ending evinces a tonal shift, a change of subject and form. The rest of the poem is crafted of long, Whitmanesque lines. In them, Roethke heaps up images—shimmering trees, blackening salmon, the body of a whale—as he tries to rouse himself from despair. Then at the end, we get this short stanza, the last two lines of which are names that roll around like candy in your mouth. The poem ends in a different language. The stanza is a four-rung ladder out of melancholy.

Poetry, because of its adroitness—you can cut very fast between centuries, images, levels of diction—allows for such leaps anywhere, but it's unusual when they happen at the end of a poem, as they do here.

3. AN INTERRUPTION. What if you wrote a crazy poem about marriage, with lots of gorgeous images in it (proving you are a good poet), with a husband as the kingpin, the thinker, the keeper who keeps a wife busy among pots and pans? The wife occasionally, unthreateningly, jots two-line ditties on the back of shopping lists (thus satirizing you, the good poet). You would have written Mina Loy's "The Effectual Marriage, or the Insipid Narrative of Gina and Miovanni." It goes on for thirteen stanzas describing this sweetly poisonous union, in which Miovanni hones his ego every night as he might sharpen a pencil. Gina devotes herself to sugaring his tea. After so many lines, it's clear the relationship, and the poem, aren't going anywhere new. Time to end. Here are the final stanzas:

> The scrubbed smell of the white-wood table
> Greasy cleanliness   of the chopper board
> The coloured vegetables
> Intuited quality of flour

Crickly sparks of straw-fanned charcoal
Ranged themselves among her audacious happinesses
Pet simplicities of her Universe
Where circles were only round
        Having no vices.

(The narrative halted when I learned that the house which inspired it
    was the home of a mad woman.) (66)

If the poem had closed with "Having no vices," it clearly would still be satire. After all, Miovanni is "Magnificently man," in his library, while Gina, in hoop skirts, wipes up after him. She hasn't even enough imagination to visualize a circle—a coffee stain on a table—as a metaphor, say a tarnished wedding ring. (I love Loy's implication that women poets know circles aren't merely circles.) True, Loy could probably have gone on for more stanzas writing wonderful phrases like "audacious happinesses." Instead she cuts off the narration with a footnote.

The final stanza is like Loy throwing down her pen. I can't stand it anymore, she seems to say. I can't stand writing one more line about this couple I am so skillfully skewering; it's driving me mad. The shift in point of view, and from lineated verse to prose, underscores that Loy means us to hear her voice, not the narrator's.

4. AN OPEN BOX. George Oppen let a fair number of his poems trail off with ellipses. Witness "The Bicycles and the Apex." It's about how mechanical things—gadgets, gears—are not the pinnacle of our culture, as they were in ancient Rome, but merely props among its demise: gauges and ratchets to fix tires in slums and barren suburbs. Yet Oppen, a master carpenter, surely never fell out of love with machines. The final ellipsis in the poem hints at his ongoing romance with tools, subtly undermining the poem's idea that salvation by invention is no longer possible:

But we loved them once,
the mechanisms. Light
and miraculous . . . (106)

Other times, in Oppen, a punctuated poem has no end stop. "The Forms of Love" is one such. A couple walks through a field to what seems like a lake but might also be fog. The landscape has different possible forms, as the lives of the pair do as they fall in love (the poem is about a night shortly before Oppen would elope with Mary Colby). In the last stanza, the enjambed "Ringing under the stars we walked" turns the lovers upside down: their feet are in the sky. Notice the unpunctuated last line, which has the effect of suspending the couple in the medium of memory, almost as if they're in space.

> Beginning to wonder
> Whether it could be lake
> Or fog
> We saw, our heads
> Ringing under the stars we walked
> To where it would have wet our feet
> Had it been water (106)

The lack of end stop allows the poem to retain the shape-shifting power of memory. The field is very close to being water; it might even be a different substance, such as pure light. The open ending also lets the speaker hover relatively close to the long-ago night. It's an old recollection, but not a distant one.

Now imagine the poem with a full stop. That final period would seal the poem off in the present, as if to say: We thought the field was water, but the field definitely was *not* water. The end.

5. A SURPRISE ENDING. Patricia Carlin's "The Box Turtle" is essentially a four-stanza description. It starts by offering facts: The turtle can live for up to a hundred years and has no voice. It moves "inch by rickety inch over the yellowing leaves." Next comes a precise account of tail, legs, and head, after which the poem begins to indulge in increasingly fancy, figurative language: the shell is an "intricate, tessellated bone-house." The turtle's body is a "soft self" poking out to observe the world, then withdrawing. Still, technically it's all a description of the creature. Here is the last line:

> And there is no metaphor in this. No poetry. (3)

No poetry, Carlin says. Yet there is music in her many images. And there are, in fact, metaphors: the red on the shell is "profligate," the "soft self" could easily stand for the poet. But there is no hint that the poem is heading toward a grand pronouncement about poetry, that it is an anti-ars poetica. "Here's how not to make a poem," last line says. Ironically, the abrupt shift at the end makes the poem a poem. Up till then, it had been a carefully composed description.

"The Box Turtle" is one in a line of poems with surprise endings, most notably "Archaic Torso of Apollo," by R. M. Rilke. You might be familiar with its parting salvo. After four stanzas describing a Greek statue, in which the headless torso seems to stare at the reader, and not vice versa, Rilke ends with the imperative: "You must change your life." James Wright's "Lying in a Hammock at William Duffy's Farm in Pine Island, Minnesota" is a rejoinder to Rilke's poem. Wright's poem is a short list of one-line descriptions: butterfly, shadow, sunlight, hawk. He ends by declaring: "I have wasted my life." The poem suggests observation isn't enough, which is the same thing that bothered Roethke about being a poet. Carlin, for her part, says that description, never mind observation, isn't enough to make a poem a poem, or a person a poet.

Of course, it is hard to sense when a poem is enough of a poem, or whether we as poets, while writing, are enough of a poet. That's one reason why poets unconsciously rely on repetition at the ends of poems. We want to make something, and to have finished making it. "Beauty is truth, truth beauty" pulses like a metronome. It has authority. The rhymes and slant rhymes at the close of old formal poems—"Gently thy fatal scepter on me lay, / And take to thy cold arms, insensibly, thy prey" (Finch 562)—seem to ask for a contemporary free-verse counterpart in the form of repeating words, which themselves are a sort of identical rhyme.

In most of our waking hours, though, poets are between poems. If we try to think of ourselves that way, then perhaps more of our poems might be allowed the modest (yet compelling) goal of bridging one place with another, rather than creating a closed universe. There might be less pressure to End, and our ears and minds might not long so much for the familiar, reassuring click of the lid shutting. Right? Right.

Works Cited

Ansel, Talvikki. "You Don't Know What Happened When you Froze." *The New Young American Poets*. Ed. Kevin Prufer. Carbondale: Southern Illinois UP, 2000. 4. Print.

Bang, Mary Jo. *The Bride of E: Poems*. Minneapolis: Graywolf, 2009. Print.

Carlin, Patricia. *Original Green*. New York: Marsh Hawk, 2003. Print.

Ellis, Thomas Sayers. "Practice." *The New Young American Poets*. Ed. Kevin Prufer. Carbondale: Southern Illinois P, 2000. 58. Print.

Finch, Anne. "To Death." *The Norton Anthology of Poetry*. 5th Ed. Ed. Margaret Ferguson, Jon Stallworthy, and Mary Jo Salter. New York: Norton, 2005. 562. Print.

Friman, Alice. "Getting Serious." *The Best American Poetry 2009*. Ed. David Wagoner. New York: Scribner, 2009. 26. Print.

Hass, Robert. "Vintage." *Human Wishes*. New York: Ecco, 1989. Print.

Katz, Joy. *Fabulae*. Carbondale: Southern Illinois UP, 2002. Print.

Kercheval, Jesse Lee. "[The ice does not melt]." *New Letters* 75.4. Ed. Robert Stewart. Kansas City: 2009. Print.

Lehmann, Rebecca. "A Dream of The Road." *Drunken Boat* 11 (2010): *N.p.* Web. Winter 2010.

Lerner, Ben. *Angel of Yaw*. Port Townsend: Copper Canyon, 2006. Print.

Loy, Mina. "The Effectual Marriage, or The Insipid Narrative of Gina and Miovanni." *Others: An Anthology of The New Verse*. Ed. Alfred Kreymborg. New York: Knopf, 1917. 66. Print.

Mackowski, Joanie. "Boarding: *Hemaris Thysbe*." *The Best American Poetry 2009*. Ed. David Wagoner. New York: Scribner, 2009. 78-79. Print.

Oliver, Mary. "Red." *The Best American Poetry 2009*. Ed. David Wagoner. New York: Scribner, 2009. 93-94. Print.

Oppen, George. *New Collected Poems*. New York: New Directions Press, 2008. Print.

Parker, Alan Michael. "No Fool, The God of Salt." *The New Young American Poets*. Ed. Kevin Prufer. Carbondale: Southern Illinois UP, 2000. 135-136. Print.

Roethke, Theodore. "The Longing." *The Far Field*. Garden City: Doubleday, 1964. Print.

Scott, Winfield Townely. "Poem At Christmas," "Four Poems." *New Letters* 75.4. Ed. Robert Stewart. Kansas City: 2009. Print.

Sharma, Prageeta. *The Opening Question*. New York: Fence, 2004. Print.

Smith, Barbara Herrnstein. *Poetic Closure: A Study of How Poems End*. Chicago: U of Chicago P, 1968. Print.

Sutton, Pamela. "Forty." *The Best American Poetry 2009*. Ed. Davis Wagoner. New York: Scribner, 2009. 123-124. Print.

Swensen, Cole. *Goest*. Farmington: Alice James, 2004. Print.

Volkman, Karen. *The New Young American Poets*. Ed. Kevin Prufer. Carbondale: Southern Illinois UP, 2000. Print.

Wright, Charles. *Sestets*. New York: Farrar, 2009. Print.

Yee, Debbie. "Cinderella's Last Will and Testament." *The Best American Poetry 2009*. Ed. David Wagoner. New York: Scribner, 2009. 146-147. Print.

Contributors

ROBERT ARCHAMBEAU's books include the poetry collection *Home and Variations*, the study *Laureates and Heretics: Six Careers in American Poetry*, and the edited collections *Word Play Place*, and *The &NOW Awards*. The recipient of grants and awards from the Academy of American Poets, the Illinois Arts Council, and the Swedish Academy, he is professor of English at Lake Forest College.

STEPHEN BURT is professor of English at Harvard. His books include *The Art of the Sonnet*, with David Mikics (Harvard UP, 2010); *Close Calls with Nonsense: Reading New Poetry* (Graywolf, 2009); and *Parallel Play* (poems) (Graywolf, 2006).

MARY BIDDINGER is the author of *Prairie Fever* (Steel Toe Books, 2007), the chapbook *Saint Monica* (Black Lawrence Press, 2011), and *O Holy Insurgency* (Black Lawrence Press, 2012). She is the editor of the Akron Series in Poetry, and co-editor of *Barn Owl Review*. She is an associate professor of English at the University of Akron, and directs the NEOMFA: Northeast Ohio Master of Fine Arts consortium.

MICHAEL DUMANIS is the author of *My Soviet Union* (University of Massachusetts Press, 2007), winner of the 2006 Juniper Prize for Poetry, and the co-editor, with poet Cate Marvin, of the anthology *Legitimate Dangers: American Poets of the New Century* (Sarabande, 2006). He teaches at Cleveland State University, and serves as director of the Cleveland State University Poetry Center.

ELISA GABBERT is the author of *The French Exit* (Birds LLC) and, with Kathleen Rooney, *That Tiny Insane Voluptuousness* (Otoliths). Gabbert's poems and essays have recently appeared in *Colorado Review, Denver Quarterly, Open Letters Monthly, Pleiades, Sentence*, and other journals. She lives in Boston and blogs at http://thefrenchexit.blogspot.com/.

JOHN GALLAHER is the author of four books of poetry, most recently *Map of the Folded World* and *Your Father on the Train of Ghosts* (with G. C. Waldrep), as well as the chapbook *Guidebook* from Blue Hour Press. He's currently co-editor of *The Laurel Review* and lives in rural Missouri.

ARIELLE GREENBERG is co-author, with Rachel Zucker, of *Home/Birth: A Poemic*, and author of *My Kafka Century, Given,* and several chapbooks. She is co-editor of three anthologies, most recently *Gurlesque* with Lara Glenum. She is the founder-moderator of the poet-moms listserv and is an associate professor at Columbia College Chicago.

JOY KATZ is editor-at-large for *Pleiades*. She is the author of two poetry collections, *The Garden Room* and *Fabulae*, and co-editor of the anthology *Dark Horses: Poets on Lost Poems*. She teaches in the creative writing program at the University of Pittsburgh. Her awards include the Nadya Aisenberg Fellowship at the MacDowell Colony.

DAVID KIRBY is the author of *Talking About Movies With Jesus* and other books of poetry. His latest book, *Little Richard: The Birth of Rock 'n' Roll* (Continuum, 2009), was hailed by the *Times Literary Supplement* of London as a "hymn of praise to the emancipatory power of nonsense." For more information, go to www.davidkirby.com.

ELIZABETH ROBINSON is the author of several books of poetry including the National Poetry Series winner, *Pure Descent*, and the *Fence* Modern Poets Prize winner, *Apprehend*. She was a 2008 Foundation for Contemporary Arts Grants to Artists Award winner. Her most recent book is *Also Known As* (Apogee Press).

BENJAMIN PALOFF is the author of *The Politics*, a collection of poems, and has translated several works from Eastern and Central European literatures, most recently Marek Bieńczyk's novel *Tworki* and *Lodgings: Selected Poems of Andrzej Sosnowski*. He is a poetry editor at *Boston Review* and teaches at the University of Michigan.

CRAIG SANTOS PEREZ, a native Chamoru from the Pacific Island of Guahan (Guam), is the co-founder of Achiote Press and author of two poetry books: *from unincorporated territory* [hacha] (Tinfish Press, 2008) and *from unincorporated territory* [saina] (Omnidawn Publishing, 2010).

NICK STURM is a student in the NEOMFA: Northeast Ohio Master of Fine Arts. He is an assistant editor of the Akron Series in Poetry, poetry editor of *Rubbertop Review* and associate editor of the Akron Series in Contemporary Poetics. His reviews and interviews are forthcoming in *Barn Owl Review, The Laurel Review,* and *Whiskey Island.*

COLE SWENSEN is the author of thirteen volumes of poetry and sixteen book-length translations. A PhD in literature from U.C. Santa Cruz and a 2007 Guggenheim Fellow, she's the founder and editor of La Presse Books and is on the permanent faculty of the Iowa Writers' Workshop.

MICHAEL THEUNE is the editor of *Structure & Surprise: Engaging Poetic Turns* (Teachers & Writers, 2007). His poetry, essays, and reviews have appeared in numerous publications, including *Jacket, Pleiades,* and *Poets on Teaching: A Sourcebook* (Iowa, 2010). He teaches English at Illinois Wesleyan University.

MEGAN VOLPERT's fourth book is *Sonics in Warholia* (Slack Buddha Press, 2011). She is co-director of the Atlanta Queer Literary Festival, and a high school English teacher with an MFA from Louisiana State University. Predictably, www.meganvolpert.com is her website.

MARK WALLACE is the author of more than fifteen books and chapbooks of poetry, fiction, and essays. Most recently he has published a short story collection, *Walking Dreams* (2007), and a book of poems, *Felonies of Illusion* (2008). He teaches at California State University San Marcos.

Index

Hierarchization, 10
Hill, Jessie, 107
Hittinger, Matthew, 39
Hofmann, Michael, 86–88
Hollander, Jean and Robert, 85
Hollander, John, 65
Hollywood, Amy, 93
"Homage to Creeley" (Spicer), 96–98
Home and Variations (Archambeau), 22n
Homer, 60, 62, 85
"Homo Faber" (Bidart), 82–83
Horace, 81
"Horn o' Plenty, or Notes Toward a
    Supreme Cornucopia" (Parker),
    35, 38
"How Can It Be I Am No Longer I"
    (Brock-Broido), 31
Howe, Fanny, 98
How to Stop Time (Marlow), 106, 108
HTML Giant (blog), 2, 40
Hubbard, L. Ron, 87
Huey "Piano" Smith & The Clowns, 107
Humorless hybrid (Theune), 129–32
"Hybrid Aesthetics and its Discon-
    tents," 4, 117–47; "Against Unity"
    (Wallace), 119, 120–29, 149;
    "Gurlesque" poetry, 133–37; humor
    and hybrids (Theune), 129–32;
    Language poets *vs.* Official Verse
    Culture, 117–19; response to,
    148–53; whitewashing American
    hybrid aesthetics (Perez), 137–40
Hybridity, Lowe's definition of, 138
"Hybridity in Gurlesque Poetry"
    (Greenberg), 119, 133–37
"Hybrid" works, 118

I

"If Thou Dislik'st What Thou First
    Light'st Upon" (Young), 52–53
"I Had My Headphones On" (Parker),
    36
"I Have a Dream" (King speech), 46
The Iliad, 105
Illogical Causation, 39–40
Imagery in poetry, lack of, 104–16
Immanent concept of meaning, 117
Immigrant Acts (Lowe), 138
Indistinctness, 104–16
"Infants Corner" (Kasischke), 70–71
In medias res, as poem ending, 159

Intention, direct reference to, 104–16
Intentional Ambiguity, 36
Interruption, as closure technique,
    161–62
The Iowa Anthology of New American Poetries
    (Shepherd), 118, 120, 125, 130
"*Iowa delenda est!*" (Hall), 6
Iser, Wolfgang, 107
"Is I Another?" (Lauterbach), 101
"Is That All There Is?" (Lee), 107

J

"January 28, 2003" (Spahr), 55–56
Jarman, Mark, 48
Jarnot, Lisa, 45–46, 51, 67–68
Jesus Christ, 87, 88
Job, 100–1
"Jock-A-Mo" (Crawford), 107
Johnson, Ronald, 83
Johnston, Devin, 7576
Jonson, Ben, 59–60
Joubert, Joseph, 88
Jubilate Agno (Smart), 46

K

Kasischke, Laura, 69–71
"Kasmir" (Leon), 34
Katz, Joy, 4, 154–65
"Keeping Things Whole" (Strand), 39
Kiberd, Declan, 24
Kim, Geraldine, 136
King, Ben E., 109
King, Martin Luther, 46
King James Version, 79, 87
Kinnell, Galway, 81
Kirby, David, 3, 104–16
"Kiss by the Hotel de Ville" (Doisneau),
    111
Knox, Jennifer L., 52
Koch, Kenneth, 50, 53
Koran, 87
Koschmider, Bruno, 114
Krupat, Arnold, 137
Kuipers, Keetje, 75
Kulakov, Vladislav, 82

L

Lancashire, Ian, 76
The Last Professors (Donoghue), 25
Lauterbach, Ann, 92, 101